TO KENT

AN EXTRA OF
MENTOR, AND COACH...
WERE "THERE", WHEN I
NEEDED YOU THE MOST!

FOREVER THANKFUL —

[signature]

10/12/16

JUST
DO
THESE
FEW
THINGS

**How to Find and Develop Exceptional
Talent, Share the Wealth, and Build a
Great Company and Culture**

Jeffrey Rowe

For information about this title or to order other books and/or electronic media, contact the publisher:
Jeffrey Rowe
4642 Ridge Road
Cincinnati, OH 45209
www.nunanvogelrowe.com
jrowe@nvrcinci.om

ISBN: 978-0-692-75200-5

DEDICATION

To my wife, Anne, and our four great children – Emily, Matt, Kate and Maggie. May I someday be able to adequately repay you for all the sacrifices you made so I could do my "thing."

TABLE OF CONTENTS

FOREWORD

I f you picked up this book, there is a good chance you may be looking for ways to help your current or future business reach new levels of success. Or perhaps you are looking for ways to identify great workplaces.

As you can likely guess from the title *(Just Do These Few Things: How to Find and Develop Exceptional Talent, Share the Wealth, and Build a Great Company and Culture)*, this book is based on the concept that company culture – the behaviors and beliefs that guide how company employees interact with each other – has more to do with a company's long-term success than its products or market.

Author Jeffrey Rowe measurably proved this concept by advancing the financial performance of a reasonably successful company to the next level. And, you should bear in mind we are talking about a company that operated within a fairly low-profile market niche (chemical dispensing), a business space not normally associated with dynamic growth.

When Jeff joined Hydro Systems Company in 1998, it was one of Dover Corporation's smallest business units and was mostly unknown within the Cincinnati community. He and his team grew it into one of the most profitable among all of Dover's business units, while at the same time making the company more of a known presence within Cincinnati, a place of employment that was highly sought after by some of the top talent within the community.

While you may not have heard of Hydro Systems, I can assure you that, were you to talk with employees (or the families of those employees) who worked for the company during Jeff's tenure, you would hear a common, positive theme. With very rare exception, they would tell you that they had never worked anywhere else where they felt as valued, and where – together – they felt such a sense of true success and achievement.

As Jeff emphasizes, he believes that prioritization is one of the most critical fundamentals underlying business success, and he has written this book using this principle. In these pages, Jeff covers the seven "things" he feels were the most impactful to the success that he and his teams achieved in business, while also noting a few more principles that played a role. All seven things were vital to the culture he created at Hydro Systems, but they do not paint a complete picture of the culture experienced by everyone who chose to become a part of this great company.

How did this culture manifest itself? Obviously in many ways, but some of the most important ones were:

- Employees were engaged *at all levels* of the organization

- Employees had a good understanding of the financial performance of the company and realized that "profit" was not a bad word

- Employees were comfortable seeking out anyone else within the company for help and advice

- Employees fostered an enthusiastic, winning attitude and an expectation of success

- Customers and suppliers viewed themselves as true partners and sang our praises to others within the community

When Jeff asked a few of us – those with sufficient tenure at Hydro Systems to fully appreciate the company's unique culture – to critique his book in advance of publication, we found ourselves "hung up" around a common question: Is doing the seven things enough to duplicate the kind of transformation we achieved at Hydro Systems?

The initial and logical conclusion to that question is "No," as there are simply too many things that each and every employee does while on the job to contribute to the overall culture of any company.

After thinking further, however, we turned that question around a bit and asked ourselves, "Could a company follow through on the seven things and *not* create the kind of culture we had at Hydro Systems under Jeff's leadership?" We came to the conclusion that leaders who instill the seven things in their organization will, through natural inclination, do the other things required to create a rich, positive culture.

In short, we have come to believe that if you implement Jeff's seven things, you *will* create a behavioral and organizational momentum that instills the kind of positive culture we experienced at Hydro Systems for 17 years under Jeff's leadership.

I wish you the courage to do so.

—Stephen Vogel
Hydro Systems Company, Chief Financial Officer, 1998-2015

WHAT TO EXPECT
FROM THIS BOOK

The results of my many years of work and study, learning about leadership within manufacturing environments, are contained within this little book for you to read and absorb as you wish. I have tried my best to boil down what I have learned to a few rather simple, yet powerful, rules for running a business the "right" way. You may agree with and want to adopt many of the practices and philosophies that are shared within these pages. You may completely disagree with others and choose to ignore them. It is my bet, however, that because you picked up (or were gifted) this book in the first place, you are likely to find much of it confirming to how you are *already* leading within your own company.

Over the balance of this book, I will lay out for you the fundamental principles that I found to be the most crucial in building a successful business at Hydro Systems Company and for our parent company, Dover Corporation. Does this make me an expert on leading and operating manufacturing businesses? Certainly not. After all, it's one company, one set of circumstances and people, one point in time. If you want to learn from business tycoons who have run multiple, giant, global manufacturing operations, then you have come to the wrong source. Go read Jack's book. Or Lee's book. Read someone else's stuff, someone with far more years and much more diverse leadership experience than my own.

But if you believe that the fundamental principles for running a great company just might be unbound by size or type of business, and you believe that assembling the right group of people, treating those people with respect, and sharing the rewards of the collective effort with *all* employees appears worth investigating, well, then – what the heck – read a few more pages. I'll bet it proves worthwhile.

—Jeffrey Rowe
September 2016

ACKNOWLEDGMENTS

As I suspect is always true, my personal philosophy around the right way to run a business has been influenced by many people and events throughout my lifetime – both prior to, and during, my business career. For this reason, I had originally chosen to begin my book with a detailed description of those people and events, believing that they deserved "first position" in my story. As with many things in my life, however, it took an outside perspective to set me straight. In this particular case, my brilliant editor Ann Weber provided that perspective. Ann convinced me that the philosophy-shaping stuff about which I felt so strongly *did,* in fact, need to be acknowledged – but that the acknowledgment fit better at the end of the story than at the beginning.

After much thought and discussion, I came to agree with Ann that potential readers might be less interested in learning about the key influencers in my personal life than they would be to hear about ideas for growing and improving businesses. And so, somewhat reluctantly, I have moved the *Acknowledging the Influencers* section of this book to the end.

For those of you who (like me) tend to assign a large share of the credit for any success you have achieved in your career to those who taught you important lessons along the way, please feel free to skip ahead to the detailed acknowledgment section, read it first, and then return to absorb the rest of the text. Ann will forgive you.

INTRODUCTION

This is my first book. Also, I suspect, my last. There are many reasons behind this prediction. Principle among them is that writing a book is really, really hard.

I didn't start my life journey wanting to become an author. I am a manufacturing guy. I like making stuff. Committing words to paper, at least for me, borders on torture. I would far rather be sitting down with you and your staff in a small and crowded conference room – prototype parts, coffee cups and empty Diet Coke cans strewn about the place – than put you through the misery of reading one more business-improvement book.

Problem is, writing this down and publishing it is the only effective way to get my ideas about business, and running a company for the benefit of *all* the employees of an enterprise, into the hands of a reasonable number of people and in a reasonable period of time. I simply can't visit enough conference rooms to get the message across fast enough. I have too much else I want to do before I stop working. Goodness knows I am ready *now* to stop writing.

This book is written with two primary audiences in mind. First and foremost, it is written for business owners and senior managers who are searching for ways to grow their businesses and make them more profitable. But this book is also for developing leaders, in the hope that the lessons described here might provide helpful perspective for you as you advance in your own careers. Regardless of which audience you might fit, I hope you will be able to take some of the thoughts offered within these pages and apply them to make your own situation (and that of those with whom you work every day) a little bit better.

So, then, here goes…

Anyone who has ever worked with, for, or around me will tell you that I am a very passionate person. Passionate about developing great talent and growing businesses, passionate about treating employees (*please* don't insist that we continue to refer to them as "associates" or other such new-world dithering names) like family, and passionate about doing the right thing. And I have a deep and passionate belief that, if more companies conducted their business in the way we ran our manufacturing firm for more than 15 years, then American business could begin to embark on a new, prosperous and revolutionary cycle. Yes, I meant to say "revolutionary"!

Revolutionary in terms of operating our businesses so that everyone who works in, or touches, these enterprises wins – including suppliers, customers, employees and owners. One where we fundamentally change the way employees are paid and rewarded for the contributions they make toward improving the business and making it great. And one where everyone working within your business raises the level of urgency with which they attack their work, as well as the level of ownership and passion they feel (and express) for it.

I know it can be done, because my team and I did it. The principles required to create such a business are fairly easy to explain, and, I believe, can be implemented by any company in any industry sector. All that is required is a willingness to take risk, the guts to buck convention, and a firm dose of determination to implement these principles. But they *can* be implemented. And, believe me, if you can successfully apply them, then everybody can, and does, win.

Allow me to explain.

I began my business career with two giants of industry – The Procter & Gamble Company and General Electric. I ended the most recent phase of my work life with another large and complex public company – Dover Corporation. I learned many valuable lessons in my time spent at these three great businesses. I also learned that (at least at times) it could be difficult to remain true to my own, personal passions and belief system while working for large, public companies. It's not that large companies are bad places to work – some of my closest friends have had wildly successful careers at places like GE and Procter. And Dover is absolutely chock-full of vibrant and successful leaders I was proud to refer to as my peers during the 17 years I worked for the company.

It's simply that the inevitable (and very real) need to focus on stock value and on satisfying the Wall Street analysts' community, can lead to an over-weighted focus on short-term results. And this focus can, at least potentially, get in the way of running a business for the benefit of all constituencies – something I believe is the real key to unlocking the maximum potential of any company. This does not mean that large, public companies cannot adopt an "Everybody wins" attitude; it just means they have to work extremely hard if they want to pull it off and still keep the analysts at bay.

This short book lays out my personal business philosophy, which I developed through my years working in various manufacturing company environments, and which really came together in full measure over my years at Hydro Systems. It centers squarely on treating people with respect and helping *them* to help *you* unlock the business potential to which I refer. When you have digested the seemingly simple and straightforward lessons contained within this book, I hope that you will consider yourself to be better positioned to join the revolution – to begin to guide your company down the path of increased riches, and job satisfaction, *for everyone!*

PART ONE

The Most
Important Things

FIRST THINGS, FIRST

Those who have worked most closely with me throughout my business career will tell you that I am a zealot for prioritization. This is driven by my fundamental belief that there will always be more opportunities to grow and improve a business than there will be time to work on those opportunities. If you accept this premise, then you must also believe that, in any competitive market, the guy who gets there first will be the one who capitalizes on the opportunity the most. I, for one, believe this to my core. And that is why I am a prioritization nut.

Don't give me 10 great sales opportunities that you *think* you might have a chance to close this quarter. Give me two, and make them the most impactful two within your territory. Then put all of your efforts into getting those two closed. Bring 'em home. Book 'em. Record the wins. After that, let's talk about the next two.

It is with this same zealot mindset that I chose to prioritize the things I will share with you in this book. So while even *I* am not anal enough to worry about whether Thing #7 trumps Thing #6, or Thing #6 trumps Thing #5 (after all, they are *all* important to strive for if you truly want to drive success in your business), I would ask that, should you become determined to give up and stop reading at some point, please do so after slogging your way through the top half of the list.

And the list begins with my favorite, time-proven, number-one way to guarantee business success.

HIRE ATTITUDE AND WORK ETHIC

Everything else can be taught.

Ron was an energetic, hard-working, willing learner when we first met. But he wasn't quite as quick-minded as some others whom I had inherited on my brand-new staff. Others on the team often arrived at answers a step or two before Ron did. To his great credit, Ron was not blind to his circumstances, and he realized that, if he wanted to get ahead at the company, then he was going to have to work a little harder than the others in his department. And, most importantly, *he knew that I knew* his shortcomings, but also that I was willing to work with him to overcome them. I made it clear to Ron that I had faith and trust in him and fully expected that, with the right level of effort, he could build a successful career with our company.

And he did! From the first day Ron worked for me, he made it his mission to outwork and out-effort everyone else in his department. He kept a consistently positive attitude, never complained about the long hours he felt he needed to work to keep up with the others, and produced great results for the business. Ron's peers, seeing how diligently he was applying himself, adjusted their own level of effort and attitude to match, and so Ron's undying work ethic actually lifted the performance of the entire group. Now, *that* is a win-win circumstance!

Ron had a long and successful career with our company, and, I am certain, accomplished more than he would have ever imagined possible on that first day we met. Even more gratifying, many others throughout the company grew to view Ron with high levels of respect and admiration for the way he approached his work. Ron stands out from most with whom I have been associated over my career, as a wonderful example of attitude and work ethic winning out in the end.

William never gave serious thought to college, although he was certainly bright and intuitive enough to have success at that academic level. He likely would have had a highly successful college experience. But, for reasons known only to William, he chose to leave home immediately after graduating from high school to find his way in the working world. After experimenting with several low-paying jobs within the food-service industry, William learned about our company through a friend. He interviewed and was given a position in our factory, where he assembled a variety of different models of dispensing equipment within a small manufacturing center, working alongside a team of fellow assemblers.

William immediately impressed management and was soon promoted to a factory leadership role, and, eventually, to lead our shipping department. It was from that position that William was first noticed by the leader of our Customer Service group, who was blown away by his natural intelligence, superior work ethic and positive "can-do" attitude. William was promoted again, this time to a position within Customer Service, where he drew rave reviews from our clients by helping them to efficiently and accurately place orders, solve problems and troubleshoot dispenser issues via the telephone.

When an opportunity arose for William to be considered for a new pricing analyst position within the company, his boss and those around him encouraged him to apply for the job. It turned out that, among other things, William was a self-taught computer whiz and an expert at manipulating data and building the type of spreadsheet tools required to get a better handle on our pricing. Working with direction from two vice presidents within the business, William created one of the most sophisticated and effective pricing platforms within all of Dover Corporation.

Our business quickly began to realize improved results due to William's efforts, observed through much improved gross margins for many of our products. Margins improved by nearly 10 percentage points during the first five years William was in the new job, resulting in a huge boost to company profits, and to profit-sharing for all of William's teammates in the company! William became somewhat of a folk hero in the business as a result of the profit improvements he helped to drive. And he even began visiting and consulting with much larger Dover companies on the use of the pricing methods he had created at our company. Not bad for a high-school kid who stumbled on our business through a friend, just a few years back.

———

As I hope these stories demonstrate, Thing #1 is #1 for good reason: You simply can't have a great company if it's not populated with enough great people. And great people, almost by definition, have positive attitudes. They are also, with rare exception, willing to work extremely hard to make the company successful. It is quite plain to me, from my 35+ years of business experience, that attitude and work ethic trump education and experience, virtually every time.

If I have learned one painful lesson from my many years in business, it's that you simply can't convert someone who is fundamentally negative in attitude to positive. At least not without expending an extraordinary amount of effort trying to fundamentally change—even (essentially) rewire—what's inside that person. And, frankly, there are too many people in the world with great, positive attitudes for me to want to spend any more effort trying. Doesn't mean it's impossible. Doesn't mean it can't be done. It only means I am not wasting any more time on people who refuse to think about things in a fundamentally positive manner. We all have far too many other, much more important, fish to fry. Let our competitors try to take that hugely talented but morale-killing jerk and try to turn him positive. We are going to choose, instead, to disassociate with him.

And, as much as I believe that you can't teach a fundamentally negative person to be positive (or convert an instigator into a collaborator), I believe even more deeply that you can't teach a fundamentally lazy person to work hard. That type of behavior needs to be learned early in life. And if a person failed to learn those lessons while they were growing up and maturing, then I find it hard to believe that I am going to be successful driving a deep and lasting personality change when they show up at the doorstep of my business. At least, not without an extraordinary and horribly tiring effort. Same story applies here as with poor attitudes. There are too many good ones out there in the pond. Throw the lazy fish back!

And here's the real key: I have discovered that when you run your business this way, and take deliberate steps to avoid bringing negative or poorly motivated people into your company (and when you do all that you can to remove those that some-how snuck in the door), you will experience a noticeable lift in morale across your entire workforce. Because, guess what? The things that we want as business leaders match up quite well with what the majority of our employees also want—to work with and around others who share a can-do, positive attitude, are open with their knowledge and feedback, and work well with others.

This is not some revelation from on high, and it's not rocket science. Great, talented people like to be surrounded with others like themselves. And, they don't, and *won't,* put up with car-rying the weight for a bunch of hangers-on—no more than we would, as leaders!

So, the next time you find yourself faced with a hiring dilemma and are considering a candidate with a proven and demonstrable positive attitude and work ethic, but a not-yet-fully-developed skill set for the precise job requirements, do yourself a huge favor and defer to Thing #1. Hire them. Immediately. Just like you, they know and understand that they have shortcomings. And, because they know—and they know that you know—I suggest that if you give them the chance, they will reward you with effort and loyalty beyond your wildest expectations. Even years later, by the way, when they have completely mastered their trade and are producing the work of multiple people within the company!

I'll bet, at this point, that some of you are nodding your heads in agreement. Maybe even patting yourself on the back for your bias toward hiring great people into your businesses. And that's fabulous, because it takes a lot of exceptionally talented people to help a company grow and reach its fullest potential!

But I need you to be completely honest with yourself. How many times have you passed over a candidate who was advancing up the experience curve in their career, simply because he or she did not possess exactly what your Human Resources team had identified within the job description as a "critical" skill set? Despite his or her demonstrated history of accomplishment, attitude and work ethic? Or worse, you made decisions to hire highly talented candidates, with fully developed skill sets for the position being considered, *despite* having concerns about their attitude, teaming skills or emotional intelligence?

The plain fact is that it is darn hard for those of us in the for-profit business world to avoid making these types of hiring mistakes. But we need to commit to learning from our mistakes. We need to turn on its head conventional wisdom about hiring for specific skills and experience in favor of a relentless search for candidates who possess something far more important in the long run—great attitude and work ethic.

OK, you might be thinking, sounds simple enough. But the real trick, from my experience, is instilling the right mindset in your senior-management team around this philosophy of hiring. Once your senior team is convinced that hiring for attitude and work ethic is the priority, they will design the systems required to allow this mindset to translate into hiring practices. Their direct involvement in designing the systems that support this way of hiring will give them an opportunity to demonstrate their buy-in to others in the company. Through their own hiring actions, they will make it obvious to everyone in the organization that they now put attitude and work ethic at the very top of the list.

Of course, the home run when searching for key hires is finding the complete package—a candidate with a great attitude and work ethic along with a fully developed skill set. Those people are out there, but—no big surprise—they tend to be in great demand (as they should be). Which leads us to Thing #2.

THING #2

CONTINUALLY SEARCH FOR THE BEST TALENT IN YOUR MARKET

And be willing to pay for it.
Then find a home for it in your organization.

om came to our business from a somewhat unique background, having spent his entire career working within the field of professional baseball. When I first met Tom, he had just been displaced from his position in player development with the Cincinnati Reds, and he was considering a move to another club, in another city. Tom and his wife were both from Cincinnati, and their great young family had grown up there, so they wanted badly to remain in the area. Problem was, the Reds were, quite literally, the only game in town.

Some of Tom's friends encouraged him that he had talents transferable beyond baseball, and they helped him to begin networking around the city. I met Tom as a favor to a friend – something we did a lot at our business.

17

I was immediately impressed. Tom demonstrated a strong sense of maturity, exhibited great personal presence, and struck me as a natural leader of people. I told him that I thought he might make a very effective senior sales person, key accounts manager, national accounts sales guy, etc. I told him, further, that while we did not have any such position open at the company, I still wanted him to come over and meet some of my team. And I also told him that we often hired talent without having an immediate position into which we might deploy it. This was because we recognized just how rare truly exceptional talent can be in today's competitive market, and how important it is to building business success. Tom agreed to come over and meet the staff.

It came as no surprise to me that Tom loved my team and that the team loved Tom. We made him an offer to come to work for us on a one-year, special trial basis. The agreement was this: If Tom discovered, during the one-year trial, that he enjoyed selling but did not like our business model, then we would help him find his next sales job elsewhere in Cincinnati. Conversely, if, after one year, Tom came to like our business but dislike selling, we would look for something else for him within the company.

It is important to note that the deal we agreed upon held no guarantees for either party, and we acknowledged to one another, going in, that each side was taking significant risk. But were we, really? In fact, what Hydro Systems was getting in this deal was the use of a highly talented individual, driven to prove himself and perform. And Tom was getting an environment in which to perform, with a company willing to give a talented individual the chance to prove that he could successfully learn a new trade. The arrangement worked, because both the company and the candidate felt a close spirit of commitment for making it work, as well as a strong sense of trust for one another.

We shook hands on the deal and started Tom in a regional sales manager's role. It was a position that would typically pay well below the compensation level we offered Tom to get him to join our company, but one that gave him the best chance to learn our business, our products, and to evaluate life as a salesperson. And we had faith that Tom's talents would find a long-term fit somewhere on our team, in a position that would more closely align with the compensation we had offered to get him onboard.

Fast-forward five years, and I'll bet you can guess the rest of the story. Tom became Hydro Systems' North American Sales Director, responsible for a team that accounts for roughly half of the company's annual revenues. He was widely recognized and admired by his peers, subordinates and senior management as one of the foundational talents within the company, and he was even considered for higher-level roles elsewhere in Dover. All because we took a mutual chance on one another. And because we stayed true to Thing #2 by recognizing, being willing to pay for, and making a place within the organization for a great talent. Talent, by the way, that was coupled with absolutely exceptional attitude and work ethic. A perfect parlay of Things #1 and #2!

Ted was a very successful, high-energy marketing and sales leader for a valuable and fast-growing customer. He rose through the ranks of his employer, first as a regional sales person, then sales manager and business unit manager. When I met Ted, he had already accomplished a great deal in his career, and he had been – not surprisingly – well-compensated for his efforts. I made a mental note that, should I ever hear that Ted was unhappy with his work circumstances; I would talk to him about coming to work for Hydro Systems.

As fate would have it, his employer passed over Ted for a key position just a few years after our initial meeting, and he and I talked about his concerns with how the situation had been handled. Knowing that Ted was already quite well-paid, and probably not affordable to my company (even given our willingness to apply "stretch" standards), I offered to help him with his networking efforts should his frustration ever reach the point where he made a decision to leave his employer. In time, Ted did choose to make a change, and so he and I met to discuss what other companies in Cincinnati might be of interest to him. During our meeting, I also asked Ted if he would consider doing some short-term consulting work for a division of our company while he conducted his job search. He agreed.

The more our people worked with Ted, the more they were impressed. His ability to see and consider all aspects of complex commercial situations, then cut right to the heart of the matter and develop the best solution for the customer and the company, was rare. Within just a few weeks, I had a parade of folks walking into my office to tell me that we had to find a way to hire Ted. While I chose not to confide in any of them, I knew that Ted's pay range was so far beyond our company's norm that it would be next-to-impossible to make that happen.

One afternoon, while talking with Ted, I casually chose to broach the topic with him. He surprised me by saying that he had never enjoyed working with a group of people more than he did at our company, and that he would be willing to take a substantial step back in pay to come to work for us. While this could bring Ted's compensation closer to what others in the company made for doing similar work, he would still stick out like a sore thumb. And, of course, there was risk that others might discover what Ted was making and, therefore, feel slighted.

After mulling things over, I brought our CFO and HR leader together and told them that I wanted to reach out (I mean, *really* reach out) and extend an offer to Ted, on the basis that talent such as his simply doesn't come along very often. They wholeheartedly agreed and we got Ted onboard, essentially creating a position in which to start him. As you might guess, within just a few years, Ted had been promoted multiple times and was well on his way to moving toward an executive-level position with the company. And the payback on his efforts for the business was nothing short of spectacular. A perfect instance of having the courage to reach out to hire the best talent, then watch as they overdeliver!

Note that these two examples underline the importance of all three of the major, underlying themes associated with Thing #2 – search for the best talent, compensate accordingly, and find a place for it. In fact, if any of the three had not been imbedded within our culture, then we would very likely have missed out on bringing these two key contributors onto our team in the first place.

For example, if we were not 100 percent committed to continually and proactively invest the time required to seek out the best talent in the marketplace, we would never have met Tom and Ted. And if we had remained stubbornly tied to traditional, structured salary ranges, instead of adopting a mindset to pay what it took to acquire the best talent, we would never have enticed them to come to work for our company. Finally, if we were unwilling to look beyond our list of official job openings at the time we met Tom and Ted – and to think creatively about how we could either find or create a position for them within our organization – we would never have given either a second thought. And in doing so, we would have passed over an opportunity to bring two incredibly talented, high-impact people into our company – individuals who paid back our investment in them multiple times over.

As I believe these examples clearly demonstrate, in business (as in other aspects of life), we generally get what we pay for. There is just no denying this simple, undisputed, time-proven truth. Exceptional talent, as we all acknowledge, is extremely hard to find. It also happens to be the single, biggest difference-maker to building business success. When you are fortunate enough to find it, *hire* it. And teach your folks to be constantly trying to find it.

OK, now time for some honest self-reflection. While we can all cite examples such as these from our own work experiences, most of us, when faced with a hiring decision for a key position within our companies, still struggle to stretch out in order to meet the compensation needs of the best available talent. We still tend to, somehow, convince ourselves what a particular position should be "worth," and then reject any candidate – no matter how talented – who does not fit neatly in the pre-established range for the job.

Why is this so prevalent?

There are many reasons, of course, but they all amount to excuses in my book. Too often, we allow the compensation "experts" within our businesses to dictate the rules for hiring, which can effectively lead to tossing out the best candidate for a job, simply because he or she doesn't match up with the payroll slot we have established for the position. Our history of often finding good talent "within range" predisposes us to believing that such a strategy is always the right one. This type of thinking, in my view, is misguided and ignores the tremendous impact that the exceptionally talented candidate can have on your business and its financial results. We have all faced these choices in our careers and know that – virtually without fail – when we stretch out for the best available talent, we are almost always well rewarded with great performance. Often, multiple times over.

That senior sales guy, accountant, engineer or operational leader who costs you an extra $10,000-$15,000 per year above the defined pay range for the position will produce *double* the results, compared to the guy your HR leader or CFO want you to settle for, just because they "fit the range" for the job. We all see it, know it, experience it, and yet somehow choose to ignore it when making key hiring decisions!

At Hydro Systems, we organized our entire company around searching for, finding, vetting and hiring the best talent we could find. Beginning with the senior leadership of the company (and led by me), we spent a disproportionate amount of our time in networking activities with our peers in the local business community, spreading the word about the great environment we were creating at Hydro Systems, and letting anyone who would listen know we were on a constant and relentless search for talent. And not just talent to fill current job openings. Talent that could help our company grow, in any discipline.

As the people with whom we networked began to understand more about our company and culture, and as they watched us make the type of unconventional hires described in the stories above, the community started to take notice. We quickly developed a reputation as both a great place to work *and* a magnet for exceptional talent.

In order to effectively deal with the many talented individuals who began flowing our way, we developed and refined best-in-class processes around vetting and hiring candidates. This way, we ensured that only the best among those whom we considered for joining our business would ever make the cut. We conducted structured team-screening techniques, taught our key managers effective behavioral interviewing skills, made use of outside testing resources, and always insisted that multiple, senior leaders at least one level above the hiring manager approved of the successful candidate.

Folks who interviewed at Hydro Systems went home tired, but also fully informed and fully vetted. And we always took the attitude (and communicated it clearly to the candidate) that the thoroughness of our process was designed to benefit them as much as ourselves. We recognized that if we made a "bad" hire and had to correct our mistake down the line, it was something the company could recover from, with time. But for the candidate (about-to-become-new-employee), it could represent a true disaster. I mean, who wants to be back on the market only one year after securing their new job, attempting to explain to the next potential employer why they experienced such a short stay with their last company?

By taking this attitude, we generally were able to ensure that the fit was right—for both the new employee and for us. And we saved ourselves, and the candidate, a lot of future business interruption and heartbreak. Following these processes, and maintaining this attitude, allowed us the very best chance for finding enough of the right talent and for making very few mistakes on new hires.

We did one other very interesting thing at Hydro Systems that I bet some of your companies also do, with or without actually recognizing it. We created an "Executive Vice President of Culture." Her name was Margaret, and her real title was "Manager of Customer Service," but she was, essentially, anointed as our head of cultural fit. I liked to refer to her, playfully, as our lead "culture cop." Since we hired lots of people for our factory workforce in order to keep up with our rapid growth over the years, we recognized that we needed to insert someone into the direct labor-interviewing process who could inject a test of "fit" into the process. Margaret was nominated, and she gladly accepted the new role, on top of her customer-service leadership duties.

We all know folks like Margaret. She was that rare employee who, although she worked for the company for 30+ years, somehow always managed to adapt her style and work habits so that she kept up with the ever-changing business demands. And she had an innate ability to meet and talk with a candidate and know immediately whether they would fit into our hardworking, share-the-load culture. You could not BS Margaret, and it didn't matter how many glowing stories you told about what you had accomplished in your previous jobs. If Margaret spent any amount of time with you, she could quickly develop a true sense for your attitude, work ethic and sense of teamwork. She was the first screen for each potential factory hire (and for many office candidates, as well). If you couldn't get Margaret's stamp of approval, you wouldn't even be given the opportunity to interview further. We saved an extraordinary amount of time in the hiring (and firing) processes by putting our culture cop at the front of the chain.

———

I hope that, by now, some of this is sounding familiar to many of you. After all, we all like to claim that we hire only the best talent. I bet you make that claim, too. But are you really doing it or just pretending to do it? Because this is one area where we simply can't give lip service to the process and then expect to achieve great results! We need to ask ourselves the really tough questions concerning our hiring practices, exhibit leadership and courage, and follow our instincts.

Tear up the old rules around salary ranges and job definitions. Institute a process of continuously searching for the best available talent within your market spaces. Pay the money required for the best available talent when you find it. And identify opportunities to install a vetting process that's centered on cultural fit ahead of all else. If you do these things, I believe that you will run your business with fewer—but far better—employees, for years to come.

THING #3

SHARE THE WEALTH WITH ALL EMPLOYEES

Design ways to tie their financial well-being to that of the business.

L
arry lived in Clermont County, a rural area on the far east-side of Cincinnati, and a good 50 miles from where our company headquarters was located. Living in what most people would refer to as "farm country," Larry was anything but well traveled. He also was not highly educated, at least not in the formal sense. But Larry was street smart, and he was inventive. He started working for us on our factory floor. Larry's extraordinary work ethic and positive attitude, however, quickly earned him a series of significant promotions. By the time I arrived to run the company in 1998, Larry had advanced all the way to Shop Superintendent.

Larry could be accurately described as a typical "Hydro guy"—hard-working, loyal, always willing to lend a hand. He wasted little time or effort, and he demanded the same behavior from the people in the factory who worked with and for him. What this meant to me, as CEO, was that motivating the people in the factory to get customer orders out the door – within the time frame promised, and in accordance with specifications – was drop-dead easy. In fact, it was far easier than at any company where I had ever worked.

A little more explanation would probably help.

Those of us who have grown up within the manufacturing sector know the month-end drill quite well. We have gotten used to having factory leadership come to us at the end of each month, hat in hand, and with a host of reasons (excuses, really) as to why certain orders could not ship. Oh, how we all hate those dreaded, but seemingly inevitable, last-minute surprises! I am no different than the rest of you, and although I was conditioned to this month-end game, I still hated it. Imagine, then, my surprise (and delight) upon arriving at Hydro Systems, where I discovered exactly the opposite dynamic in place. I have to admit that I struggled, at first, to adjust to this new dynamic – one where manufacturing leaders (like Larry) approached me at month-end, pleading with me to help get customers to agree to accepting shipments *early*.

What in the world was driving this heretofore (at least for me) never-experienced and absolutely urgent focus on shipping not just on time, but ahead of schedule? The answer lies in the genius method for compensating employees that the founders of the company had instituted, years prior to my arrival at the company – a "one-for-all, all-for-one" extraordinarily generous profit-sharing plan. And while I could not take credit for creating the system, I darn sure worked hard to keep it in place.

At Hydro Systems, I quickly found out that any time we needed to find a way to respond to a customer in need, we could simply summon Larry to our offices and discuss the customers' requirements with him. It didn't matter whether the customer had erred and forgotten to place his orders on time, or if he had failed to accurately forecast demand, or if he just got a much bigger order from *his* customer than he had expected. The only focus in these discussions was on how we could get the order built and shipped within the timeframe that the customer had requested.

You see, Larry knew full well that he would not have to twist any arms to get his people to work a little overtime, or to give up part of an evening or weekend with family, to come in and build product for the customer. His folks in the factory already recognized that a share of the profits resulting from this type of extraordinary service came right back to them. And so, whenever we needed them, our people, literally, lined up to help.

Unlike at any other company where I have ever worked, Hydro Systems employees never had to be told *why* they were being asked to sacrifice for the customer. Larry's people, and all of the others in our business, knew that they were helping to create a responsiveness edge that differentiated our company. And they understood that our ability to consistently out-respond our competition created intense loyalty among our customer base. Our customers knew that we could (and would) pull them out of any jam into which they might get themselves. We simply delivered where others could not. And, at base, it was the company's share-the-wealth attitude, delivered via profit-sharing and driving the everyday actions of people like Larry that allowed us this huge competitive advantage.

———

Now, let's get something straight, as we talk further about sharing the wealth of a business enterprise with all of the employees in the company. I am not so naive that I believe profit-sharing is some sort of radical, new concept. Or that such disbursement plans represent breakthrough thinking in the world of employee compensation. In fact, variations on such plans have been around for many years – certainly in manufacturing, and also in other company settings. At another company where I worked earlier in my career, we had an extremely lucrative "piece-part" incentive for the machine operators in the factory. Unfortunately, that program actually drove focus toward local-area optimums and individual efficiencies, not to overall team "wins." And for each year I worked at P&G, they awarded shares of company stock to the employees – a nice reward, but not very closely tied to anything I might be able to impact to help grow profits from my position in the company.

Unlike with those and many other profit-sharing programs, the way the Hydro Systems' founders built their company – right from Day One – was deliberately intended to tie each individual employee's financial rewards *directly* to overall company success. The profit-sharing system at Hydro Systems was designed to make employees feel and behave like owners of the business, and we did everything in our power to reinforce and celebrate this principle.

We held quarterly meetings with the entire employee group to review the most recent business quarter and year-to-date results, including summary financial information. And we emphasized what the various employee groups could do to impact those results and the corresponding payouts they received from the profit-sharing pool. We talked continuously about the overall strategy of the company and how individual employees could support that strategy in their day-to-day jobs, emphasizing each person's fit in helping us move toward our desired, long-term direction.

We went out of our way to explain to engineers, customer-service reps, sales people, accountants and factory workers specifically how their individual efforts could impact service to our customers, and thereby, our profits. And we never missed an opportunity to hammer home the impact that all of the little things we did for customers came back to benefit us in the form of future orders and better pricing. We celebrated improvements to factory and office processes, and to materials-purchasing programs that expanded our product margins. We made certain that we publicly recognized those individuals responsible for the improvements.

The employees we recognized for these profit-improving actions took on instant hero-status with their peers, who realized they were getting a bigger profit-sharing check due to these efforts. As more and more of our folks began to see and accept the tie between their individual performance and company profit, behaviors began to change. Our people started taking time to stop and pick up loose parts around their work areas on the factory floor and to return them to the proper bin (not the trash). They suddenly realized that those parts represented nickels and dimes of cost to the business, and that lots of nickels and dimes can add up to real money! They begged us *not* to replace employees who left the company, doing everything in their power to show us they could spread the work and pick up the additional load.

They took time to stop their work and engage with customers who came to visit the company, and to express their thanks for the business with which they had honored us.

They did all of these things because they now recognized how lower costs, happy customers and fewer people (spread over the same or greater profits) could impact their personal earnings, their sense of control over their own fate, and what they could provide for their families.

The system instituted by the founders at Hydro Systems for sharing the wealth has worked, and worked well. And it has stood the test of time—for more than 50 years!

I would advise any CEO or business executive wanting to make truly significant improvements in performance to take a hard look at how people—all people—are compensated within their company, and to think honestly, and creatively, about how you can better tie employee compensation to company results. Having seen it work to build true employee loyalty and create substantial, tangible, competitive advantage, I can think of no more impactful method for getting *everyone* in your business pulling in the same direction.

I challenge you to invest the time and energy and to think hard about how you might create something similar inside your company. Then find a way to make it happen. It may be difficult, and you will likely have to develop a thoughtful and staged plan to transition the compensation systems in your company to a truly impactful profit-sharing basis. But if you are successful, you will create a virtual flood of employee engagement that will help to differentiate your business from those with whom you compete—for years to come.

THING #4

ENCOURAGE AND PROMOTE CONSTRUCTIVE CONFLICT

Teach the art of effective confrontation.

Sam was, quite obviously, not happy. He sat at the table without muttering a word, but his expression said it all. Debbie was in the middle of a presentation about how she planned to reorganize the inside sales group in order to better align her employees with individual customer groupings. Sam sat politely and said nothing, but it was clear that he disagreed with the new, proposed structure. To make matters worse for Sam, most everyone else on the staff was joining enthusiastically in the discussion and offering Debbie their support for the new plan.

Trouble was, only Sam understood that Debbie was overlooking the impact the new organization would have on communications between the office and the factory floor, and he was imagining the disaster that would soon ensue as the newly created customer-aligned positions began communicating, individually, with his shop-leadership folks (rather than through one central liaison, as had been the tradition). And guess what? Sam was right. We were standing on the precipice of a communications nightmare that would have brought the factory to a literal halt, had we not backed up and had more discussions before proceeding.

Roughly three-quarters of the way into Debbie's presentation, I could see that Sam was clearly not buying the new organizational concept, so I asked him, very directly, what he thought. At first, he did the politically correct thing and said he was "just fine" with it all. You see, Sam did not want to embarrass Debbie in the meeting environment by pointing out what he saw as the shortfalls in her plan, and he sure did not want to start an argument with the other members of the staff, most of whom seemed to be so fully in agreement with Debbie.

So I forced the confrontation.

I told Sam that, while he said he was "just fine" with the proposed changes, I suspected from his body language that this was not at all the case. And I told Sam that I felt it was his responsibility to "call the baby ugly," if that is what he was truly feeling. Sam was somewhat embarrassed that I would call him out like this in front of the others. Debbie seemed stunned that I would encourage someone to openly criticize her ideas. Sam initially resisted arguing his case, so I embarrassed him a bit further by telling him that he was doing nobody any good by sitting on his thoughts and allowing the company to proceed down a path with which he, quite obviously, disagreed strongly. Now it became really uncomfortable in the room. I knew we were finally making some progress!

With a little further encouragement, and after hearing a speech from the boss (me) about everyone's responsibility to speak up, argue if necessary and be heard on key business issues, Sam finally took the bait. He voiced his very serious concerns about the new plan's impact on communications and how strongly he felt that it could lead to serious complications within our operations.

Then he became quiet, as did everyone in the room.

After a minute or two of horribly uncomfortable silence, I asked Debbie to please answer and address Sam's concerns, as best she felt she could. To everyone's surprise, she pushed back, but in a way that offered some alternatives to her original plan. Alternatives that would allow her to capture the customer-service improvements she wanted, but that would also allay Sam's fears relative to the communication links between shop and office. The others on the staff soon joined in the conversation and many other helpful suggestions were put on the table, discussed, and adopted or discarded. In the end, we had a much better plan for going forward and a staff who had learned that confrontation, handled the right way, is a good thing for any business!

Now let's examine, for a minute, how else this situation might have been handled. Certainly there are other, more traditional, approaches that might have been tried and which would have involved less conflict and discomfort. For example, many of us, when faced with this sort of difficult and uncomfortable circumstance, might respond by "pulling Sam aside" and having a private conversation with him to determine what was bothering him. The problem with this (often used) approach is that we lose the teachable dynamic of the moment, which I believe hugely benefits the rest of the group in the meeting. And we likely delay the resolution of the real problem by having to schedule yet another meeting, on another day, to return to the issues that could have been resolved in the initial meeting. Days, even weeks, can go by while we avoid the public conflict and try dealing with it privately in a way (as I hope you will agree) that represents a far less effective means for dealing with the conflict at hand.

OK then, many of you may be thinking, how about I set up a separate meeting with just Sam and Debbie to "settle their differences"? You know the drill. Get the two of them "offline" and we'll settle this thing. Except that such an approach, once again, sacrifices the team dynamic and the learning process, and it causes even more delays in getting matters resolved—all in the name of reducing conflict. Seriously?

Finally, were my main interest in simply avoiding conflict, I could have chosen to just ignore Sam's poor behavior during the meeting and thereby "punish" Sam for his lack of maturity. How about I just allow Sam to sit and stew and to say nothing during the meeting? And then make him live with the consequences of a poor decision by Debbie and the rest of the (well-meaning) staff. I think you can see how this "solution" is really no solution at all.

The moral of this particular story: Learn to tackle conflict as a team, to do it in the moment, and to turn it to your advantage. Teach your staff and your people to attack the elephant in the room and to deal with the discomfort that comes along with doing so. It's *productive discomfort*, and they need to recognize it as such and learn to leverage it.

Go ahead and challenge each other's ideas within meeting environments. Refuse to let your people do what most are used to doing (in fact, almost trained to do) in the politically correct world in which we live, by sitting there with polite smiles on their faces while thinking to themselves what a stupid idea is being proposed. Teach them to stand up, speak up, be heard and challenge the presenter. To do what's right for the business and object, for goodness sake.

Seems easy, right?

Well, we all know the answer to that one. It's anything but easy. In most businesses, we learn to respect our peers and subordinates (and certainly our bosses), and to never, ever run the risk of embarrassing our colleagues during a meeting. We learn these behaviors because we have observed, over time, that when we are seen to challenge others, then we run the very real risk of being challenged ourselves. And, heaven forbid, anyone should ever call our idea "stupid" in an open forum!

My observation is that this sort of politically correct foolishness has, somehow, become quite pervasive in most companies—to the point where no one ever challenges anyone, on anything, anymore. Instead, we sit there virtually convinced that the idea, objective or action being proposed will almost certainly fail, and yet we keep our mouths shut. This leads to disastrous results for the company because huge expenditures of time, energy and money are wasted on truly bad ideas, to which—simply by the law of averages—millions are given birth in the business world each day!

So then, what's the solution?

I believe the answer is actually a very simple one. But like teaching and demanding teamwork among your staff or any subset of managers in your business, it is some of the hardest work you will ever take on. Still, you *must* take it on, and you must teach the art of what I like to refer to as "effective confrontation" if your business is to reach its maximum potential.

I had a boss at GE who pounded this seemingly simple idea into my head, quite early in my career. He was a firm believer in that age-old adage about business-meeting dynamics: **Until it becomes a little uncomfortable in the room, we are not really making any real, significant progress toward solving the issues at hand.** This is, of course, due to the collective strength of the thoughts and ideas of any group of individuals compared with the singular strength of just one, no matter how loudly (even intimidatingly) that one idea might be expressed. I have seen this theory proven time after time during the years I worked in manufacturing businesses and attended thousands upon thousands of meetings. It's a fact: Until each member of the team is allowed, encouraged, cajoled, even *forced* to weigh in, and to do so with complete honesty relating to the issue being considered, you simply can't arrive at the best answer for the business, even in those rare instances where everyone on the team is in seeming agreement.

Teaching the art of effective confrontation, while uncomfortable at first, will have the effect of binding any team more tightly together and making key group members feel more a part of the major decisions made around your business. When I ran meetings at the various businesses where I worked, I always kept this important principle in mind. It starts by demanding of your direct reports (after all, they report to you and you get to rate them and set their salaries) that they challenge your own ideas during meeting discussions. I always told my staff and other groups of managers in the companies where I worked that I wanted them, encouraged them, to tell me I was stupid or wrong, if they really felt that way about the ideas I was proposing. And I made darn sure that everyone understood it was not only OK to challenge the boss, it was important that they do so. In fact, it was their obligation to the business that they speak up, wherever and whenever they disagreed with the voiced suggestion on any key business matter.

This does not mean, of course, that we made decisions by committee. We certainly did not. And there were times when, despite having heard from a majority of my staff the strong desire to move in one direction, I chose to take the company in quite another. After all, a CEO or business leader cannot abdicate the final decision-making authority to any group of people, any more than he or she can abdicate responsibility for bottom-line results. But the process of hearing from everyone, and encouraging constructive conflict through the discussion of these topics, led to more good decisions than bad. And the power of collective thinking, input and imagination undoubtedly kept us from pursuing some very ill-fated initiatives for our business.

As with teaching leadership, I firmly believe you will find that once taught well (and taught consistently) at the senior-leadership level of your business, this is a process that can be appropriately cascaded down within the organization. Once your second-level managers see you encouraging those who report directly to you to openly and enthusiastically criticize your own ideas, and to argue aggressively with you for what they feel is best for the company, others will begin to get it. And the culture of effective confrontation for the betterment of the business will take firm and fast hold. Just don't fool yourself into thinking it will be easy to take those first steps. You must acknowledge that it's difficult, it's a journey, and it has to be led from the top of the organization. If you are the CEO, that means *you*!

As the ultimate leader of the enterprise, you are foundational to this process if it is to be successful. You must be willing to set your ego aside and to make yourself fair game to the process. You need to be resolute, and you need to plan and expect that some people will never become comfortable with handling conflict as we have described it. And that's OK. They just can't work at the most senior level of your company! To accept less from your top executives is to sell your company woefully short.

Dig in, do the hard work and get started with the process. I promise you, the results will be remarkable.

10 PERCENT OF THE PEOPLE IN THE WORLD ARE BAD FOR YOUR BUSINESS

Accept this as fact, and always strive to be certain these people work for other companies.

Joe was not happy. As a matter of fact, he was quite upset with several of his peers on my staff. We were sitting in an off-site meeting to discuss and assess the performance of all salaried employees within the company, something we came to do within our business at regular, planned intervals. This was, however, our first such meeting, and no one on the staff had ever experienced anything quite like it.

I sensed a lot of trepidation as we prepared for the meeting, where I demanded that each staff member rate their peers' employees, as well as rating and ranking each of their own people, from best to worst. They were instructed to pretend as though they had to terminate their entire staffs, and then begin anew to fill the roles within their respective departments. Who would they add back first, second, third, etc.? Who would they add back last? Think of it like a zero-based budgeting exercise.

The atmosphere in the room was highly charged on this particular afternoon, and Joe's discomfort was palpable. His expression told the group everything they needed to know. They had upset him, and upset him deeply, with the skewering they had just given one of the employees within his group – an individual whom he had actually ranked quite highly. Joe dug in his heels and defended his employee, quoting chapter and verse about her strong performance and the splendid metrics relative to her assigned position – in this case, involving collections of invoices due from customers, as well as management of the company's credit-approval/credit-hold processes.

The problem, as Joe would eventually come to understand and accept had nothing to do with the actual work that his employee was doing. Rather, it had everything to do with the way she conducted herself while accomplishing that work. She tended to behave in a condescending, sarcastic manner, and often exhibited a "holier than thou" attitude in dealing with her co-workers. She was sometimes short, even curt, in her discussions with customers, and she showed limited flexibility in working with the sales force to keep money flowing in (and orders flowing out) with some of the company's largest and most important customers. Turns out, she was widely despised by virtually everyone with whom she worked day-to-day, and her relationships were either frayed or broken with almost every one of her internal customers.

As can often be the case, Joe was completely unaware of the poor behaviors of his "troubled" employee. All he saw were the fabulous results she was producing, results that drew consistent praise from our parent company – financial guys who absolutely loved our DSO (Days Sales Outstanding) and our past-due performances. Unfortunately, neither Joe nor the corporate guys understood the horrible impact that the employee in question was having on her teammates within the business. At least, not until the day's discussion.

As the meeting continued, and I demanded that the group continue being completely honest with Joe, it became apparent that Joe had a blind spot relating to the employee in question and her poor habits in working with others. Lacking the type of honest, open, group-delivered and discussed feedback that Joe was receiving from his peers during this meeting, he likely would have remained blind for some time longer – probably until someone in the office blew up at his employee and we had a major issue on our hands. Instead, we were able to carefully orchestrate an exit for the disruptive employee in question, much to the delight of her peer group within the company.

Joe and the rest of the staff came to understand and support the critical nature of this type of cross-department feedback as the staff got more practice with the methods employed during these sessions. After just a few meetings, everyone on the staff fully bought-in to the process. The work was hard and the feedback brutally honest – at times, even hard to digest – but everyone understood the end objective: to effectively identify those troubled players who needed to be placed on an improvement path or discharged from the company, as well as to highlight and discuss the best and brightest among the salaried staff who deserved and warranted additional development.

After everyone had been given their opportunity to weigh in at these meetings, we spent the bulk of the time discussing those people at the top and bottom of the collective lists of employees (actually far too much on the bottom, at first). And we recognized that we had many steady-performing "workhorses" who were well-placed in the middle of each department, as is the case with any company's employee population.

It's worth noting, by the way, that conventional management theory tends to favor spending the majority of your time in sessions such as these discussing development of your top talent. While I am largely aligned with this thinking, I believe it is absolutely critical that the leadership team in your company demonstrates a willingness to deal with the underperformers as a high priority – and early in the process. Otherwise, you risk losing credibility with your workforce, who witnesses leadership tolerating poor performance. Unless you learn to deal with this as a senior team, and make the really tough calls on your underperformers, the talent bar for your company will never be raised. In order to be truly effective, you need to develop strategies for dealing with all of the groups identified within your talent-review processes – the underperformers, the promotables, the superstars and the workhorses.

The type of talent-review session described above became a regular part of our fabric at Hydro Systems, and, with time, we greatly improved both the skill and efficiency that we brought to the discussions. Everyone on the staff came to realize that if they had a "bad apple" or underperforming employee working within their department, then their peers were going to call them out on it during one of these sessions. There was simply no longer any place in our company for the underperformers and bad actors to hide.

As time went on, we saw the number of underachievers and employees with either a bad attitude or poor work ethic decline dramatically among our workforce. This is because each staff member drew courage from their peers to handle any performance issues that might arise, and to deal with them in a time-efficient manner. This resulted in review meetings where we could spend progressively more time making sure we were doing all we could for those at the top of the list – our best and most valuable performers who deserved positive feedback, development time and attention – and progressively less on those at the bottom. And as we know, developing your best people feeds the lifeblood of any business enterprise.

I am certain you must be thinking, as you read these passages, that the described "weeding out" of underperformers is nothing revolutionary in a business. I mean, we all have to review our people at least annually, ostensibly to make sure the best performers get the best financial rewards, and that underperformers are dealt with appropriately. What goes unrecognized in my view, however, is the huge impact that peer feedback – properly managed and facilitated in a group setting – can have on the effectiveness of the employee-evaluation process. No one likes to be embarrassed or surprised in the presence of his peers, and an attitude of higher performance (and behavior) expectations quickly takes hold when the peer review becomes a normal part of the process.

In the end, it's up to all of us to help one another spot and deal with underperformance within our businesses. You can be certain that the underperforming employee's peers see what's being allowed to go on around them, and that they will raise a cheer (and, very likely, their own level of performance) when we take the appropriate action with our underperformers.

So stop fighting the laws of nature. Accept that some people out there are bad for your business, and that, at some point a few of them are going to sneak their way into your company. Quit ignoring the negative impact on employee morale by allowing the C performers in your business to be treated the same as the A's and B's. Instill in your staff the courage to deal with those C players, expeditiously and with a firm hand. Your entire workforce will salute you for it, and you'll reinforce the culture you need to drive improved business success. Nip performance issues in the bud and set your C's on a path to improve or exit. Your culture and your company will be far better for it.

THING #6

COMMUNICATE STRATEGY TO ALL EMPLOYEES

*Having this context will make them
far more effective at their jobs.*

Mary had just joined the company in a direct labor position. She was sitting in a conference room between Jim, a new mechanical engineer, and Josh, a new accounting clerk. Jerry, who joined the sales department just a few weeks back, had just asked a very thoughtful question regarding the company's strategy for penetrating the Asian market.

Now, wait a minute. Who in the world are these people and why in the world have they been taken away from their jobs (and their day-to-day assignments as new employees), and assembled in this room, with a half-dozen peers with whom they have never met and with whom they may never work? I mean let's be honest, Mary has never been, and likely will never be in Asia. What is she going to contribute to this discussion? And does Jim really care about what's happening halfway around the world, when he has important project work waiting for him on his desk? And, finally, for goodness sake, Josh is just an entry-level accounting clerk. Why are we worried that he knows what the company is up to in China? Aren't we, essentially, wasting our time talking with these new employees about top-level company strategy, especially the part of our strategy that has absolutely nothing to do with their current, day-to-day activities?

In fact, at Hydro, we believed quite the opposite, and we assigned much benefit to making sure that every one of our employees understood the long-term direction we had for the company. We were convinced that well-informed employees, who truly grasped the big-picture objectives for the business, would be more committed to helping us achieve those objectives, more dedicated to the long-term success of the business, and—thereby—more effective in their jobs.

And so, the scene described above played out every 90 days or so at the company. We pulled together all new hires and held discussions with them, in an open, engaged, question-and-answer format, and for a full 90 minutes or so, about big-picture company strategy. The payback for this investment far exceeded our expectations, but I'll share more about that later. First, let's talk for a bit about how we approached the formation of company strategy in the first place.

———

One of the first things I did when I took over as CEO at Hydro Systems was institute a once-per-year, full-week, senior-leadership team meeting (off-site) to talk about company strategy. No financials, no near-term objectives discussions allowed. If it was tactical, then you were not allowed to even bring it up. One full working week, away from the distractions of the home office, to focus on the big-picture stuff. Each time we went way for these strategy discussions, I reminded my staff, as the very first order of business on Day One, that these were our most important meetings of our year for two reasons: 1) We were the only group in the company with the privilege to weigh in on long-term strategy and 2) The rest of the employees working in the business depended on our getting the long-term strategy right, if we were to be successful and continue to grow and prosper.

The leadership team took this responsibility very seriously. We did so because we knew that there were so many families depending on the outcome of those sessions. Not just the well-being of our own employees, but of their extended families as well. We had an accounting clerk trying to save for her son's college education, an engineer caring for his ailing parents, a sales guy hoping to take his kids on their first-ever beach vacation, a materials planner who just got hit with some unexpected home-repair expenses. All of our employees had husbands, wives, boyfriends, girlfriends, children, grandchildren, parents and other loved ones who counted on them for financial support. And those employees, in turn, counted on the money they earned at Hydro Systems to provide at least part of that support.

That meant, of course, that they were really counting on the senior management of the company—the anointed direction-choosers—to get this stuff right, if they were going to continue to enjoy good-paying jobs that would allow them to provide for the people they loved. After all, none of those hard-working and loyal employees had the opportunity to attend our meetings, and they did not get to vote on long-term strategy. Only the eight or so who participated at the senior level of the business, in any particular year, got that vote. And that is why it was easy for us to accept the truly critical importance of these meetings, and why we took the work accomplished during these strategy sessions so seriously.

The number-one rule (really a *demand* I made of the staff) at these meetings was that everyone had to speak their mind and had to do so on every topic discussed. No one was allowed to sit on their hands and agree with the ideas proposed by the loudest or most influential members of the team. These lively discussion sessions are where I believe that we really honed our skills at arguing effectively as a team. And, I also believe, it paid huge dividends for the company and all of our employees during the years I was CEO.

The strategy sessions were always full of loud, passionate, appropriately aggressive disagreements and arguments. We often fought like cats and dogs, and I forbade anyone from sitting idly by and watching others present and argue their points of view without weighing in themselves. This way, we were successful in getting all the arguments on the table and dealt with during the week we were away, and we were able to emerge from our discussions with agreement on the best way forward.

Now, don't get me wrong on this important point: Our agreement was rarely ever unanimous, but it was always effective. And once we had agreement (often referred to as "general agreement" because I was the "General"), everyone on the staff knew that it was expected they would fully support the agreed-upon direction and never, ever be seen to snipe, take shots at, or otherwise undermine what the group had decided when we all had returned to the normal, day-to-day business environment.

This was a golden rule that we always demanded be honored. And it worked well, so long as everyone truly felt as though they had the chance to voice their argument and be heard during the off-site sessions. That's why I took my role as facilitator so seriously, and I made sure to engage, even drag, each staff member into the most critical discussions. This is a classic example of the CEO demanding that his staff follow the rules of managing effective conflict, as taught under Thing #4.

When we did return to the business after our strategy weeks, we always tried to communicate, promptly and throughout all employee groups, about what (if anything) had been changed or altered relative to our long-term business plans. The employees came to expect and look forward to these communications because they reinforced the importance of having a good plan and a clear, strategic road map if we were to continue successfully growing the business. We always tried to tie the importance of having a good strategy to the financial performance of the business and to the size of quarterly profit-sharing checks – emphasizing that the employees darn well should care about strategy because it tied directly to their wallets!

We took every opportunity we had to communicate top-level strategy to our employees. Not just new hires, but the entire workforce. At our quarterly results meetings, at our Christmas celebration, and anytime we got the employees together to talk about a major change or event that significantly impacted the business. We did so because we were convinced that informed employees make more productive workers. We put outsized effort into ensuring that every employee at the company could understand, and relate to, company strategy – and to how they could help the business accomplish its long-term strategic goals. We felt a strong sense of obligation to share with our employee group clear and open communication about where we intended to take the business. This reflected the extremely strong relationship we maintained with our workforce who had willingly hitched their wagons (and bet their family's well-being) on the company's success.

The return on our investment in sharing company strategy came in many forms. For example, whenever we had an opportunity to win a new account (an objective consistent with our top strategic priority around protecting and growing our core business), it was quite easy to rally the workforce to do whatever it took to win. And when we needed people to travel and stay out-of-town (and away from their families) to help integrate an acquired company, we were overrun with volunteers because our people understood the strategic importance of acquisitions as a vehicle to growth. Likewise, when we needed help launching a new product line or closing on a big sales opportunity for one of our emerging-market business units, we had people lined up to make the trip and lend a helping hand. Time after time through the years, as we grew our business, we were rewarded with extraordinary loyalty and effort from an employee group who shared the same page with us, relative to our most important business priorities.

Pulling all of this off, of course, required that we keep the strategy as simple as possible, and so we made this one of our major tenants for both strategy creation and communications. Over time, we evolved to a strategy that centered on only four or five key points that could be communicated in very few words and which allowed every employee to see where they fit in to supporting the strategy and making the business more successful.

Our strategy was stated in language that was straightforward and easily understandable—simple words and phrases that could be referred to often and remembered by everyone in the company, regardless of their level or position. These methods worked well, and I honestly believe that a good deal of our success as a business was built on the foundation of knowledge, trust and communication around the big-picture strategic objectives of the company. This is stuff, which I argue, many business owners and managers assume their workforce either won't understand or won't care about.

If you are one of those leaders, I challenge you to take the risk and communicate more with your folks about strategy. If you do, I predict you will help to uncover productivity, enthusiasm and caring for the customer that you didn't know existed within your workforce. Begin sharing more of what you may think they just won't get, and watch what happens!

REACH PAST THE EMPLOYEE AND TOUCH HIS FAMILY

Find ways to make them partners to the company's success.

Mark was a highly sought-after Human Resources executive. At the moment, he was debating between two job offers—one from our company and another from a major, well-known, well-respected, local hospital group. Suffice it to say that the hospital position was the much higher-profile role of the two he was considering.

When Mark returned home from his final discussions with the hospital staff, his two teenage daughters greeted him, excitedly, at the front door. In their hands, they held a giant gift basket that had been delivered to Mark's home that same day. The basket was full of the type of stuff that really appeals to teenage girls—gift certificates for the movies, Chipotle and other local restaurants popular with the teen crowd; wrist bands and hair ribbons in an assortment of the latest styles and colors; chocolates and snacks; and books on fashion. The basket also contained a beautiful, live plant arrangement for Mark's wife, featuring all of her favorite floral combinations.

All of this had been cleverly compiled and delivered by Hydro Systems' Director of Customer Service (remember Margaret, our culture cop?) who had gleaned critical tidbits of information about Mark's family and their favorite things during an interview with him just a few days prior. The card that arrived with the basket said simply, "For Sue and the girls. We hope your family will make a decision to join ours." It was signed, "From all of your friends and future co-workers at Hydro Systems."

How much difference do you believe this silly gift basket made on Mark's eventual decision to accept our offer over the more financially rewarding one from the prestigious, well-known hospital?

Only everything.

You see, Mark's family had, essentially, made the decision for him by the time he arrived home that day. They reasoned and successfully convinced Mark that any company who would go to that extent to understand and reach out to his family before he worked for them, must be a darn good place to hang your hat. And so we got one of the best HR guys in town to come to work for our company, and the prestigious hospital went back on the recruiting trail.

The kind of success we had at Hydro Systems in reaching through our employees to touch their families and build loyalty beyond the norm did not happen by accident. It required that the staff of the company fully bought into all that we did in this regard, just the same as any other key aspect of our business strategy. The reaching out as described in the above story had to be handled by someone senior within our organization who was both respected and empowered by the leadership team, and who really understood our employees, got to know them and who cared. You can't fake this stuff!

This type of above-and-beyond effort to recognize and respect the families of our employees had to originate from the top of the company – with my senior leaders and myself. The person handling these types of "touches" needed to be supported and encouraged to find ways to come up with these differentiating initiatives – and to make them happen. They had to know that the company expected them to spend valuable work hours thinking of and executing ways to creatively touch our workforce's families and make them feel appreciated. And, like all things, this work could not be effective if it were pursued in isolation. We had better be doing a darn good job implementing the first six "things" if we expected Thing #7 to make a genuine difference.

John was the son of a staff member at Hydro Systems. To refer to John as a "late bloomer" would be the ultimate understatement. Perhaps because he had an older brother who graduated high school with a record grade-point average, knocked out perfect scores on both college entrance exams, and got admitted to MIT; or maybe because both his mother and father were each off-the-charts intelligent and he figured he couldn't possibly match their intellect, John grew up as a bit of a rebel. Not the best student, and not the most focused student, either. Bright as heck, but a bit, well… under-motivated.

John's attitude, and his effort relative to all things academic, drove his parents to distraction. His father, nearing his wits' end with his rebel son, expressed his frustration to me one day during a wide-ranging discussion around business and family topics. I suggested that we might have young John, then in his third year of college, stop by for a visit to discuss what he really wanted (and expected) out of his future. His dad agreed that it couldn't hurt and arranged for John to come down to Hydro Systems.

I asked several members of my staff to meet with and interview John about his career interests, and when the interviews were completed, we met to compare thoughts. We discovered that although John had not made a full effort to pursue a high grade-point average up to that point in his university journey, and although he seemed (at least outwardly) somewhat unenthused about what to do with his life after college, John actually had a lot going for him. He met well, made a great first impression, was incredibly quick and bright, and showed genuine engagement when talking with the experienced executives on my staff about career opportunities. The kid was mature way beyond his years, and he was quite comfortable trading thoughts with senior executives.

As a follow-up to this initial discovery process, John came back to Hydro Systems multiple times, and he, his father, an HR colleague and myself began to discuss career opportunities that played to his identified strengths. John quickly established an objective to obtain a career in consulting, a field that we all agreed would fit well with his strong analytical skills, his innate intelligence, and his ability to meet and converse with senior executives in a business environment. All well and good, except that John had a major hurdle to overcome – his grade-point average. Because of his somewhat lackadaisical attitude through both his freshman and sophomore years, John had a major challenge facing him if he were to improve his grade point to a respectable range by graduation. And he acknowledged that without a respectable GPA, he would have little chance of getting much traction with the type of firms he wanted to target within the consulting field.

Armed with his newfound focus on a specific objective in an occupation in consulting, John committed to raising his GPA. And, impressively, he aced virtually every one of his classes between that point and graduation. He also sought out and accepted help in learning how to network for consulting internships and summer jobs, successfully landing a couple of good ones prior to graduation. As a matter of fact, John became a poster child for learning and applying sound networking skills, and he even published a set of notes on how to network effectively that we later put to good use to help other college students in similar circumstances.

John went on to find a great starting position with a major health-care consulting firm right out of college, and since then, he has made a change to an even more prestigious firm where he is advancing quickly through the ranks. His success stands as a great example to many who have followed a similar path: It's never too late to get your act together and get focused on a goal, if achieving the goal is truly important enough to you. And with sufficient hard work and focus, any goal can be achieved!

John is only one among many dozens of employees' children whom we helped at Hydro Systems, both during and after their college years, to discover a career focus and to learn how to network in order to effectively differentiate themselves from the crowd. In fact, the college child-assistance program is one of our very proudest accomplishments at the company.

At Hydro Systems, we made a deliberate habit of reaching out to current and prospective employees and their families via means such as those described above. We did so because we recognized the powerful draw that comes from making an employee's family feel like a part of our own. In addition to the networking help and career assistance for our employees' families and close friends, we budgeted a large amount of money each year for special events that touched employees and their families. Events such as our annual summer picnic (yes, you remember those stupid things—except everyone came to ours and everyone had a great time with family, kids and grandkids), Reds baseball games (typically cost the company somewhere around 450-500 tickets and several thousand dollars in "fun bucks" for our 200 employees in our Cincinnati workforce), a wonderful Christmas celebration (complete with the local performing-arts school boys' and girls' choirs singing seasonal carols), and others events from which both our employees and their families benefitted. These events worked only because of all the other things we did right with the way we operated our business.

We did all of this because we felt it was vitally important to let the spouses, children and significant others who surrounded and supported our employees know how much we appreciated their family member who worked with us. We went out of our way to express that appreciation, and we did it on a repetitive basis.

And talk about return on investment! Many of our employees joked that they couldn't even think of quitting work at Hydro Systems for fear that their families would divorce them! And, in reality, their jokes were not too far from the truth. We all talk about the importance of building employee loyalty, but hearing the expression of those sentiments from family members made us feel as though we had truly nailed that objective.

We deliberately stretched the limits of the employee/employer relationship (in a good way) when we felt it was the right thing to do for our employees, their families and for the company. An expensive, over-the-top basket of gifts for the family of an employee whose spouse was facing a particularly difficult surgery, for example. Or finding representation for the child of a highly regarded, long-term employee suddenly facing legal trouble, and then helping with the costs. We even helped an employee or two with threatened foreclosures on their homes, and we regularly leveraged our local networks to provide referrals to some of the best doctors in the city, when our employees' families did not know where to turn. Truly unusual, above-and-beyond efforts, where we felt they were warranted. And certainly not the norm for most companies.

Why don't more companies understand the power associated with reaching through their employees and trying to touch their families in a positive and engaging manner? It certainly can't be the expense. The money we spent annually on the types of programs described above absolutely paled in comparison to the return we received in loyalty and work effort from our employees.

Could it be that many executives, in the current business environment, think these types of efforts are old-fashioned or are simply not effective with today's more worldly and sophisticated employees? If that's the excuse, our evidence certainly implies that such thinking is dead wrong. Maybe business owners and executives are just too caught up in the day-to-day pursuit of ever higher sales and profits, and don't allow themselves sufficient time to stop and think about how employees might respond if the company made that extra effort to touch, appreciate and thank their families.

Whatever the rationale (read: excuse) might be, I suggest that companies are missing a huge opportunity to get the maximum effort and loyalty from their workforce if they are not making a sincere effort to reach through the employee and touch the family. I am strongly biased on this point because I have seen first-hand the powerful effect of doing just that, in consistent and creative ways. I strongly encourage you to give it a try!

PART TWO

Some Additional Stuff

A Word of Introduction

When I start my next business venture, I intend to design it around teaching and reinforcing the things discussed within the previous chapters. I am convinced if more businesses focused on doing these few things, and on doing them really well, we could change the world of business as we know it. More people would arrive at and come home from work happy, find true purpose in the many hours spent at work each week, and have the opportunity to enjoy financial security beyond what they thought possible. It will be my fundamental mission, for the rest of my working life, to teach business owners and managers these lessons in the hope they will adopt at least some of them.

I intend to weave a few other "things" into the fabric of my next venture, as well, although these ideas are more commonly written (even preached) about in today's conventional business practice than some of the topics discussed in the preceding chapters. Things which, while often pointed to as keys to business success, simply won't have the same impact unless you implement them within a company culture already resting upon the concepts discussed in the preceding chapters of this book. I have seen these additional actions make a real difference in how people think and feel about coming to work, every day. And because I have seen the impact they can have on a company and its workforce, I have chosen to share them here.

DEMAND, TEACH, CONSTANTLY REINFORCE AND REWARD TEAMWORK

Your personal behavior around teamwork will drive others to follow.

Mary was one of the most brilliant and capable marketing minds with whom any of us had ever been associated. She held undergraduate and post-graduate degrees from one of the nation's most prestigious universities and had a long history of success with Fortune 500 companies. Our company had been lucky enough to grab Mary a few years prior to my arrival, and it would not be overstating the truth to say that she had it all, including a quick wit and the ability to think strategically about the right direction for the business. Only one problem: Mary was a horrible teammate.

Smarter than anyone in the room and quite willing to project or outright claim it, she often upset those around her with her arrogant behavior. No point was too small to argue for Mary, and she insisted on continuously demonstrating her superior intellect to others. And, like many who share her personality type and high intellect, Mary was smart enough to be sure never to behave badly in front of her direct boss. This behavior further eroded the trust within the leadership team, and it reinforces why Thing #4 is so critical to establishing a high-performance culture: You have to deliberately ask for and receive feedback about employees, such as Mary, if you are to spot the cancers within your organization and remove them.

Needless to say, in time we chose to separate from Mary after repeated attempts to get her to understand the negative impact that her behavior had on those around her. Her brilliance and strategic abilities simply could not overcome the growing negatives associated with having her around. Mary has since moved on in her career, and I understand she is doing well in a consulting capacity, something perhaps better suited to her style than a position where she has to continuously work closely with, and attempt to influence, a group of peers at the senior level.

———————

Mary's story is, of course, not at all unique in today's business world, where everyone talks about the importance of team-work but so few choose to demonstrate and reinforce it. We all know brilliant people who just don't understand, or refuse to accept, the value of teamwork as it impacts long-term business success. Patrick Lencioni, one of my favorite business authors, captures this lesson quite effectively in his classic book *The Five Dysfunctions of a Team*.

The book is a must-read, in my opinion, for anyone aspir-ing to senior leadership because the evidence keeps flooding in:

If you don't have a wholly functional and effective team serving at the executive level of a business, then nothing else really matters. It has been repeated often, and I firmly believe it: You can take a great team, hand them a marginally performing business, and they will work wonders with it. And, conversely, you can take a horrible and dysfunctional team, present them with a highly performing business, and they will almost certainly destroy it. We see the message play out every day in the pages of the business papers. *Nothing* trumps teamwork, and the culture built around it, in today's business environment.

So, how do you teach, train and demand teamwork within your company? As with all things, I believe it must begin with senior management. The business owners, CEO and senior leadership teams need to first invest in their own team-building efforts if they are to set the proper example and tone for the balance of the organization. While this is easy to say, I have come to recognize that it is often some of the most difficult work that is ever undertaken by a CEO and his staff. This is because any senior team, essentially by its definition, is made up of extraordinarily talented, accomplished and headstrong people. And, to be fair, those people have good reason to own these attitudes. After all, they have experienced nothing but success for most or all of their careers.

This means that most senior people can be a bit resistant to changing or adapting their management styles as it pertains to the challenge of building teamwork at the top of an organization. After all, who really believes they need to change the way they conduct themselves or their work when they have been recognized, rewarded and promoted throughout the course of their careers for those same behaviors? When tackling the very difficult work of improving team dynamics at the top, this can make for a very challenging jumping-off point.

What's a good way to get the process started? I find that gathering senior staff at an off-site location, away from the traditional office setting, makes for much more open, honest and productive discussion among the group. Nothing earth-shaking, here. We have all experienced the advantages of moving off-site for important business discussions.

Remember, however, that your first job in working with your staff to improve team dynamics is to get them to open up and to share their honest feelings – about themselves, about you and your own leadership style, and about the others on the staff and within the ranks of the company. From my experience, that difficult task absolutely demands that you take the group away from their day-to-day work environment. These discussions are anything but business as usual. Led well, they will be difficult, awkward, and sometimes even confrontational. And they will, no doubt, be quite uncomfortable for many on your staff. Trust me on this point. You will have far more productive discussions if the full team is forced together, in a remote environment, free from all of the normal workday distractions.

I also believe in the power of books, in reading and reviewing selected books together, as a staff. After all, why start from scratch when so much has already been written about improving the effectiveness of teamwork and fixing broken organizational dynamics? Beyond that, books allow you to lead discussions around new and different ways of working and relating to one another, independent of whatever specific issues might be impeding teamwork within your company.

Books allow you to separate the behavioral aspects that might be harming teamwork from the business issues pertaining to any one person's actions and arguments. Using books to teach can create a safety zone for discussions around harmful behaviors. For these reasons, I highly recommend that a CEO make a carefully chosen selection of previously documented lessons on teamwork (from both inside and outside of the business environment) mandatory reading for his staff.

At Hydro Systems, we organized a series of twice-per-year staff retreats centering on teamwork, goals and organizational strategy, targeted at building closer, more effective working relationships among the various members of my staff and myself. We often used business books on teamwork and organizational thinking to prepare for those outings. In this way, everyone came to the discussions with some commonality of thinking (or at least language and phraseology) about the team-building techniques that we planned to explore.

This method worked well, and our discussions became more productive (and a whole lot more efficient) as the years passed. This type of deliberate, focused team-building activity was, in my view, as responsible as any other factor for the growth and success of our business through the years. I see team building as vital for any business that is expected to manage significant growth and become optimally successful. The lesson here ties back to the one discussed in Thing #4, around teaching the means for guiding effective confrontation. Building strong teamwork among your key executives will help to turn destructive conflict into constructive conflict, for the great benefit of the company.

In the end, it's best stated with one of the oldest and truest of all expressions: "The guy with the best team wins." It proves out in sports and it proves out in business, as well, time after time, after time. So, tell me again: What exactly is your excuse for not prioritizing the effort it will take for you to build the best team within your company?

If you are still in need of further encouragement on this point, then perhaps you will take comfort in the knowledge that, once you have the senior staff of the company aligned and working well as a team, cascading teamwork down through the rest of the organization becomes drop-dead easy. We have all seen this work during our business careers. Once the balance of your management team observes the new, more cooperative, more closely engaged senior team working above them, they will quickly jump on the teamwork train. You can expect that they will begin asking for tools to help them learn how to interact in the changed manner in which they now see their bosses interacting. They will want to learn to behave in this same way with their own peers and with others in the business. You will need to prepare to give them access to those tools.

At Hydro Systems, we took the extraordinary step of hiring a full-time Organizational Development resource to teach team-building and team dynamics to all levels of our management—a process that most often focused on raising a manager's self-awareness through "360" evaluations and other tools that helped the manager see themselves through the eyes of others in the organization. Our OD leader taught many other skills within the realm of organizational and talent development, but team building remained a top priority for every student whom she touched.

Adding this type and caliber of resource on a full-time basis sent our entire workforce a message about the seriousness with which leadership prioritized teamwork and development at all levels of the company, effectively underpinning an entire host of highly impactful talent-development initiatives that followed. It also helped to support all that we did at the company to benefit key-employee retention. We rarely lost a key talent who was touched by the great work of our Organizational Development team.

While it may not be necessary for your business to employ a full-time Organizational Development resource, it is easy to make the argument that the expenditure of time and money will pay for itself, multiple times over. It certainly did for us at Hydro Systems.

Regardless of how you choose to teach and train the mechanics of close teamwork within your business, one fact remains beyond dispute: Until the leadership of the company commits to the importance of its *own* team dynamic and cooperation, not much progress can be made throughout the rest of your business. In my view, you really have no choice. Why not get started?

LISTEN CAREFULLY TO IDEAS GENERATED BY THE PEOPLE CLOSEST TO THE WORK

Your ability to earn their trust will drive improvement throughout the business.

And

NEVER FORGET THE MEANING OF THE FIRST WORD IN THE PHRASE "CONTINUOUS IMPROVEMENT"

Your commitment to never-ending improvement efforts will make all the difference.

I grouped these two things together because one thought readily feeds into the other. I hope you won't object. And, if you will, allow me to begin with another story...

It was the summer of 1990. I was working at Xtek, a mid-size manufacturing company that produces after-market parts for steel mill and mining applications. Business was tough. I mean, really, REALLY tough. Our largest customer was on strike. Our third-largest customer had just declared bankruptcy. We had a ton of newly acquired debt on our backs, a result of buying the company back from the LBO (Leveraged Buyout) group, Wesray Capital Corporation. In response, we had been forced to lay off roughly one-third of our workforce. What to do next?

Xtek's senior management team recognized that simply conducting our business as usual (but with fewer people) was not a good long-term answer to our problems. If we were going to survive, we needed to learn to view our business differently and to drive dramatic improvements throughout our operations. Enter a tall, charismatic, gray-haired fellow by the name of Bill Conway.

Bill was hired to teach our management group the art of something he referred to as "continuous-improvement." Bill had run Nashua Papers, where he met and became an early disciple of the famous Dr. Edwards Deming. Dr. Deming was known to generations of manufacturing and other company managers as the "father" of the modern continuous-improvement movement within the United States. Those of us in manufacturing know Deming's story: Ignored by the Big Three automakers when he tried to pitch his system for quality improvement through statistical methods. Went to Japan and taught Toyota and the other auto producers there the same thing, instead. Returned to the U.S. and was hailed as a saint and clamored over by the Big Three and many others who suddenly had to have his services because they were, now, being badly outperformed by the Japanese and others who had learned and applied Deming's methodology to their own manufacturing processes.

So this Deming disciple named Bill walks into our conference room in a suburb of Cincinnati and starts talking this strange language of "continuous improvement" to a bunch of managers who thought they already made darn good quality parts for very demanding steel mill and mining applications.

For whatever reason, perhaps because I was a younger manager and not yet fully set in my ways, I immediately saw the truth in what Bill was preaching. But, while I may have readily accepted the logic in Bill's methods, many of the more senior members of the group pushed back. And they pushed back hard. I mean, here was this guy getting in their faces and challenging every convention in the manufacturing environment—rules by which everyone had abided for decades. Bosses decide what needs done. Workers do the work, and they do it exactly the way the bosses dictate (remember, the bosses know best because they were all workers once, too), and everyone goes home happy.

Well, not according to Deming, and certainly not according to Disciple Bill. We were, instead, introduced to an entirely new, strange world order. One where, among other things, we were told to listen to and respect what the people on the shop floor (and clerks and other workers in the various office departments) had to suggest about how we could improve the way the work was done, and how things flowed through their areas of expertise. No wonder that this stuff sounded like pure blasphemy to a traditionally trained manufacturing guy.

Except that it worked.

Needless to say, our senior management team—the guys who had hired Bill and were paying him big money to change the culture and the work flow through our factories—were not about to allow the broader supervisory group to dig in their heels and reject this new way of working without even giving it a try. To their great credit, the senior staff steadfastly held their ground, reminding everyone of the many hardships that we faced in our industry, and of the harsh price of doing nothing. They were able to convince the group (although reluctantly, at first) to go along.

To this day, I have not forgotten the very simple yet eye-opening messages that Bill Conway and his staff taught us at Xtek that summer: The concept of working "on the system" instead of "in the system" if you wanted to accomplish real improvement; the idea that all processes have variability built into them. Variability that can be managed, but only with careful attention paid to the statistical truths that can be identified, tracked and dealt with in any process. And, perhaps most fundamental, the need to find answers for improving your processes with input from those closest to the source of the work, for this is where all process difficulties will manifest themselves and become obvious: out on the factory floor and elsewhere in the company, where the first-line employees do their thing, day-to-day. So simple, really, when you think about it. But so revolutionary at the time.

And, as we all discovered, not so easily done. Or at least not easily done, fast.

IT'S ALL ABOUT TRUST

The problem, as we soon understood, is that in almost any manufacturing environment (and largely because of the traditional, hierarchical system of management that most businesses had followed to that point in time), there can exist a huge, difficult to surmount, obstacle: one that stands directly in the way of enacting real process change. To understand this obstacle, you have to first remember that the poor front-line worker has been trying, for years, to get someone–anyone–in management to listen to his suggestions for improvement. And that, after a long period of frustration, he finally just gave up and stopped trying. After years of unsuccessfully attempting to influence the game, he figured out how the game was played. And he learned that he was being paid to do and not to think, to use his back and not his brain. He had long since shut down and fallen into a pattern of simply following orders.

But wait! Some strange guy shows up from New Hampshire talking in terms we cannot begin to understand, and (all of a sudden) you want me, your front-line worker, to tell you how to make things better? To actually give you my advice as to how we can improve the processes in my area and save the company money? You must be joking. Or worse, you are hiding something from me, and I suspect that it can't be good. Otherwise, why the sudden (after decades of ignoring my input) change of heart?

I believe we have put our finger squarely on the obstacle. What we have is a fundamental, deep, decades-in-the-making, trust issue. We had one at Xtek, we had one at Hydro Systems, and you will have one at your company when you first introduce CI principles to your workforce and begin asking the front-line experts how to change things to make the business run better.

It may seem obvious to you that, of course, there would be a trust issue. Yet it is truly amazing how many companies seem completely surprised when faced with employees who, after years of being ignored, don't immediately flip their attitudes to a completely trusting nature. You have real work cut out for you if you want to get serious about this CI thing. And building trust with the first-line employee groups is the place you need to start.

What are some methods we can try for building such a trusting environment? While my career has convinced me that there is no magic bullet, here are a few practical suggestions:

1. Start with *over-communicating* to the entire employee group. About the need for changing the way we all do our work. About the objectives of implementing a program of CI across the company. About your plans to get started, and your plans to ramp things up. About how, and when, you intend to educate everyone about the new tools. About what type and rhythm of communications employees can expect. And about what you believe it will mean to them, individually. Remember, this is a big deal, and you need to treat it as one if you expect folks to take it seriously.

2. Get senior management out onto the shop floor and down into the first-line working levels of each office function that you intend to attack, and do it early in the process. Let the top guys roll up their sleeves, observe and share in the completion of the actual work (wherever practical and safe), take careful notes and make lists of follow-up questions. And, yes: actually get to know the workforce on a more personal basis. You may be shocked to discover, when you engage in this type of activity, just how long it has been since anyone

in a senior-management position within the company made the effort to spend time with, and listen to, the workforce who makes all that money for you, every day!

3. Make your plans to "eat the elephant" one small bite at a time. Be clear in your communications that this is the objective. Nothing is more demotivating, even debilitating, than biting off more than you can chew and finding yourself in a position where you are unable to promptly follow up on the discussions with your front-line people – and the suggestions, both good and bad, that come out of them.

Special note: You should fully expect to get both good and bad suggestions from your people when you begin this process. You should set the expectation – right upfront – that you (management) still reserve the right to decide which ideas to adopt, which to defer and which to completely discard. You will gain immediate respect from the folks on the front line when you say an emphatic "No" on some ideas, right out of the chute. Everyone will acknowledge that not every idea is a good one, and that not all will be actionable within a reasonable range of payback for the time, effort and money required to implement them. You'll gain big credibility by not being afraid to say "No" early on in the process.

There are, of course, many other ways to attack the trust issue beyond this simple starter list. The important thing to remember is that you simply cannot get the cart ahead of the horse when launching a serious CI initiative. Until you build a sufficient level of trust in the workforce, any efforts directed toward making changes and improvements in the organization will prove to be premature and unsustainable. The good news is that if the senior team commits to spending sufficient upfront time on real and believable trust-building initiatives, you will immediately begin to see an attitude shift among the workforce. And, most exciting, you will have created an atmosphere where continuous-improvement initiatives will flourish and be welcomed (even cheered) by the employees, rather than avoided "until they go away," as has occurred so often in the past.

CONTINUOUS, AS IN "CONSTANT"

Since the invasion of the Deming disciples across the U.S. and around the world, countless individuals and organizations have, literally, made their living (and one heck of a living, in many cases) teaching the philosophy and the tools associated with CI. If we had a contest and I asked all of you to name the number of different CI programs to which you have been exposed within your careers, and the number of CI consultants whom you have met, your combined lists would, no doubt, stretch from ocean to ocean.

The world of continuous-improvement teachings and practices has become a well-established industry, in and of itself. And for good reason. Business leaders began to recognize, decades ago, that a company that did not get serious about improving its fundamental means for conducting business while its competitors were busy doing so would soon be passed by and left to die a slow death. As a result, everyone became serious about pursuing a CI program of some variety or another, with many companies jumping (unfortunately) from program to program, in search of the holy grail of CI.

But how many companies do you know that truly "get it" when it comes to CI? How many understand that CI is not about the program of the month, or the business quarter, or even a particular year when your business chooses to concentrate on operational improvement? That CI is an attitude, and one that you need to inject into as many people within the workforce as possible, if you are going to truly optimize the impact of your improvement initiatives.

I am often puzzled, when I talk with business leaders, at how many of them refer to CI as something they "attacked hard" for a period of time within their businesses. And how many cite, even with great pride, the stellar results that they were able to achieve "when they did" attack it hard. As if CI is a temporary thing. Just another set of tools and processes that need to be employed in short bursts, and only for a fixed period of time, and that can then be shelved once a specific set of targeted improvements have been accomplished.

To my way of thinking, these leaders are missing the main point of CI: You need to continuously drive your people, in all areas of the company, to focus a portion of their time on ways to simplify and improve the way work is done in their area of the business.

When you have accomplished this objective and you have engineers driving to work thinking about how to simplify a design program, customer-service folks dreaming about ways to get rid of paper documents and improve the flow of new proposals through the office, accountants thinking about ways to simplify and shorten the month-end closing cycle and how they can better serve customers through improved credit-hold processes – then you will see daily, breakthrough, business-changing improvements in all aspects of your operations. Even more importantly, your employees will feel greater ownership and empowerment to make changes they know will benefit the business. And they will derive more satisfaction from their jobs because they are not just following established processes and "doing work" each day. They are, rather, inventing new processes that save the company time and money.

It's quite straightforward, really. Better processes translate to faster turnaround. Fewer mistakes. Lower costs. More orders from more satisfied customers. Higher sales. Better profits. The cycle feeds on itself. Isn't that why someone, long ago, started your business – to meet a perceived need in the market and, thereby, make money for his family and investors? To win more customers, produce higher profits, provide for more, better and higher-paying jobs for their employees? Still sounds like a pretty good goal for the business, today, doesn't it?

From a personal perspective, I will freely share with you that this has been the major objective driving my own career. I want to do better for my family and to help others to do the same for theirs. I know I can make this happen if I am smart about where I invest my time and energy, make good strategic choices, and outwork the competition. Still, unless I have my workforce always focused on making improvements to the various operations within my business, I will risk falling behind in the race. And I don't like losing any more than the next guy. So I have to stress CI within my company, and with key suppliers and customers, in order to have the best opportunity to win.

And what's the best way to get my workforce properly focused on CI? I believe that the answer lies in the lessons contained within the preceding chapters of this book. You simply must have an engaged and trusting workforce in order to implement an effective, sustainable, companywide CI program. It all comes back to how you recruit, develop, treat, compensate and retain your employees – and how you touch their families. How you tie their personal success to the success of your business. And how you cultivate a company culture based on the lessons of *The Few Things* we just covered.

To truly optimize the results you will get out of your CI efforts, you need to first create a culture where CI can flourish. There is no piecemeal approach. You can't work on it in isolation. You can't fail to win your employees' collective trust and then expect them to take on additional challenges pertaining to business improvement. You can't have them feeling mistreated or ignored and then expect them to get excited about helping you make more money. It's human nature. If they don't see how improvement benefits everyone in the company – not just ownership or top management – you're simply not going to get them onboard.

The evidence is indisputable. CI simply can't work, sustainably, in a company with a poor underlying culture. You are going to struggle to create a good culture until you begin making sincere efforts toward establishing the business practices we have discussed as part of the foundational core of your company.

Remember, a great culture trumps the best business strategies, every time.

Begin your journey with the objective of creating the right culture. Then, when you are truly ready, you can successfully unleash the magic of CI. If you do so, you'll document impressive business successes soon enough.

SUMMARY

At the beginning of this manuscript, I mentioned that my primary objective was to document my thoughts and passions around the "right way" to run a business. And to create a medium where I could share my thoughts with as many people as possible in a time-efficient manner. As I write these concluding thoughts, I am pleased that I chose to invest the many months it took to get this darn thing done.

Having now travelled along with me, through the stories and lessons contained in the preceding chapters, I hope that you have been able to take away something of value that you can apply within the context of your own company and career. Since I began the book-writing project, I launched a new venture with two longtime business partners who share my beliefs on business philosophy and building great teams. Our new company is focused on the executive-coaching and talent-development space, and I hope to be able to use portions of this book as teaching tools within the context of this new venture.

Once we have the new business up and running, and operating on a reasonable growth trajectory, I plan to jump back into the manufacturing game via acquisition of a local company where I will have the chance to "do it all again." In my view, this will be an important step toward validating the practices

I have described within these pages—and proving their true worth. Putting these practices to work so successfully at Hydro Systems is only one instance. I believe that if I can do it again, in a different company and with different people, products and markets, then the case for *The Few Things* would become even more compelling.

Perhaps a second success will give my thoughts on business philosophy sufficient credibility that my team and I will be able to gain acceptance among a broader audience. And while I don't aspire to become Edwards Deming and I will never hold a candle to Jack Roy, the former Hydro Systems owner who set up the ingenious profit-sharing structure described in this book, I sure would like to honor them and all of the others like them who have built great businesses by following their teachings.

For now, I hope that whatever enjoyment and encouragement you take away from this book is sufficient to make you want to do a little word-spreading of your own. And that your passion for running a business for the benefit of everyone involved might now resonate within you, a bit more powerfully. Like any movement, this one will start small, and it will grow bigger only to the extent that we are able to add more disciples to the philosophy. Here's hoping that you just might become one!

Best of luck in all of your career endeavors.

ACKNOWLEDGING
THE INFLUENCERS

A t the beginning of this book, I made reference to a number of key people and events in my life that heavily influenced the way I think about business. Those influencers deserve my heartfelt thanks and deep appreciation for the lessons they taught me and the way those lessons have shaped my thinking. The most impactful of those people and events are captured here. I hope that you'll take the time to read through the list. Doing so will provide you with helpful context around my strongest-held business beliefs.

PA ROWE

The affectionate nickname that my high school and college friends hung on my father, Mark Robert ("M.R.") Rowe – a highly intelligent (31 lifetime patents), hardworking, dedicated business leader who taught me the power of a positive attitude, focused work ethic and undying support for the customer. My father was an aeronautical engineer who worked for GE's Aircraft Engine Business Group during the time I grew up in Cincinnati. In fact, he was the very first general manager of GE-AEBG's Commercial Engine Division. As the story goes, my dad's first job when coming to work for Gerhard Neuman (the recognized "father" of GE's aircraft engine business) was to find an efficient way for the company to exit the commercial-engine space. Their business at that time was all about military engines, and GE was struggling mightily with their few commercial-engine customers.

As Rowe family lore has it, my father requested some time to study and better understand the issues that had resulted in the difficulties GE was experiencing with commercial engine customers. And, he subsequently discovered, that customers very much wanted GE to remain in the business. They just needed the company to fix their problems and learn to provide better support. Mr. Neuman agreed to give it a shot, and he named my father General Manager of the then-fledgling Commercial Engine Group. This meant that I grew up with a dad who was rarely home. He traveled the world building better relations with GE customers, driving engineering upgrades and fixes, and putting into place a much-improved service organization—a role that largely consumed him until his eventual retirement.

The lesson I remember most from my father, and from the stories about my dad that I have heard from various family members and GE people, was a simple but impactful one: *Maintain an intensive, primary focus on satisfying the customer and honestly listening to what they need from you, and the rest of the decisions required to achieve success in your business will become obvious.* My father also taught me an awful lot about hard work, dedication to a cause and doing the right thing as fundamental drivers to a successful career in business. Thanks a ton, Pa Rowe.

DOUG SIMPSON

The very impressive business professional that recruited me to Procter & Gamble, and gave me my first glimpse at the difference that truly passionate employees can make for their employer. Doug was the consummate P&G man – tall, handsome, organized, well-spoken. He exuded confidence when he talked about Procter & Gamble and the great company it had become through the years. Doug was extremely proud of his company, and he very much wanted all of his employees to take pride in it, as well.

To a young man like me, just graduating college and taking his first steps in the business world, Doug was one impressive leader. When he offered me a position with Procter, there was no way I was going to consider going to work anywhere else. My singular goal, at that point in my life, was to become Doug Simpson and to do so as fast as I possibly could. He taught me the value associated with projecting "the look" of an organized, professional businessman, while also caring deeply for the company and the people you represented, and encouraging your associates to do the same. And his organization taught me how to write one heck of a great memo (a reference all Proctoids will understand).

DON WINGERBERG AND GENERAL ELECTRIC

Don was my first boss at GE. Our group, The Marine and Industrial Engine Group within GE Aircraft Engines, supported the U.S. Navy and our allied navies around the world. Don was the group's after-market sales leader. Like my father, "Wing" travelled the world taking care of customers, helping them to determine the spare parts and service packages they needed subsequent to their purchase of GE engines.

Wing taught me the value of having fun while at work, and of building relationships that helped with "internal selling," a science to which I had not yet been exposed at that point in my business career. Wing had more fun on the job than any other boss for whom I have ever worked. He had a wholly optimistic outlook on life and an infectious laugh that lit up any room. Wing never took himself too seriously, but he managed to develop deep working relationships with those around him, all of whom knew that he took the work of servicing the customer very seriously, despite his gregarious approach to life. I also learned the value of genuine teamwork from Wing, who never missed an opportunity to make one of his teammates feel great about their contribution to supporting the customer.

While at GE, I also learned a lesson that I consider, to this day, to be one of the most impactful of my career. The lesson? The *wrong* way to deal with any supervisor's most difficult job: making headcount reductions in times of crisis.

Allow me to explain.

The year was 1981. GE-AEBG was going through a really difficult time, as the impact of a recession around the U.S. became felt by virtually all sectors of the manufacturing community. It became apparent that the group was going to have to cut a lot of jobs at the huge Evendale, Ohio, plant where I was working; the headcount at the facility would eventually shrink from nearly 20,000 to about 6,500 – now, THAT is a recession). When the time came to make cuts, GE did it in the way that most large companies behaved at the time. They simply ranked their people on the basis of seniority, then cut those with the least number of years of service.

That meant that many talented, young professionals such as myself exited the business, and other, more senior employees – many of whom couldn't hit a lick (sorry, truth hurts) – remained. I told myself, at that moment in my life, that should I ever become a boss, I would not do things that same way – employing a method that struck me as completely backward in terms of providing for the long-term health of the business.

Little would I know that, within just a few years, I would be exposed to an entirely different leadership team, with a different management philosophy, who would teach me the *right* way to manage this horribly difficult and upsetting work. Thank you, GE, for putting that first, memorable peg in the ground.

JIM KIGGEN AND ART PEHRSON

My bosses throughout most of my 15 years spent at Xtek, a mid-size manufacturing company that produces after-market parts for steel mill and mining applications. This 100+-year-old Cincinnati company transitioned from family ownership to what we would now refer to as private equity, then to an ESOP (Employee Stock Ownership Plan) structure, during my tenure.

Art Pehrson was my first boss at Xtek. He had just arrived on the scene after taking an early retirement from GE's locomotive business in Erie, Pennsylvania.

Fortunately for me and for my (just informed me that she was pregnant!) wife, Anne, Art had recently visited GE's Aircraft Engine business on a recruiting mission, and at just about the same time I was being laid off. Art was looking for some young talent that he suspected might be leaving the AEBG (he fully understood the rules of the game at GE relative to seniority), and who might help him build out a more professional marketing staff at his new employer.

In my years working at Xtek, Art taught me the art of compromise (Xtek was an engineering-driven enterprise, and you had to find ways to appease the "techies" to survive within the company) and introduced me to the concept of coaching and professional development. Art helped to manage a rotational journey for me through a variety of sales, marketing and operational assignments that prepared me to follow him in his VP position upon his retirement. My first true career coach and mentor.

Jim Kiggen was CEO of the company. Jim taught me the value of community involvement and balance to work/life – he was very involved with community and not-for-profit organizations. And even more importantly, Jim taught me the "right" way to reduce a workforce when things in your business became a bit sticky.

Again, some explanation will help.

It was now 1990. Another recessionary cycle, and business conditions were slowing all over the world. To make matters much worse, Xtek had just completed its transition to an ESOP structure and had a ton of new debt service to satisfy, each month. US Steel, our largest customer, was on strike. LTV, among our top five accounts, had just declared bankruptcy. Our sales were suddenly down 35-40 percent from normal levels, and layoffs were a certainty. Oh, my. Here we go, again.

Unlike my GE experience, however, Jim led the management group at Xtek through a much more balanced, insightful and healthy way to handle the necessary job eliminations. Jim called all of his managers into a large conference room, calmly explained the circumstances facing us, and then announced that the executive staff had decided we must eliminate one-third of the salaried payroll of the company in order for the business to survive. Jim then instructed us to "rank" our people, but – importantly – to do so as if we were eliminating 100 percent of our individual staffs, and then had to rebuild our departments, one person at a time. We were told to conduct the rebuilding exercise based purely on capability, and to ignore seniority for any individual employee. Jim made it clear that he expected us to keep only the best and the most versatile, and those who would most help the business to weather the storm that had descended upon us. This struck me as truly revolutionary thinking. Here was a guy telling us to forget all about the conventional rules of seniority-based job reductions, and to, instead, do all we could to hang on to the best and the brightest amongst our staffs. What an enlightened view!

Although still a very difficult task (it is always gut-wrenching to have to tell someone they are losing their job), the management group at least had the satisfaction of looking around the company when we had finished with the layoffs, knowing that we had retained the most capable, and suitable, of our employees – giving the company the best possible chance of long-term survival. Just as important, the employees who remained in the company came to the same conclusion, thereby developing a much deeper respect for senior management. The company survived and prospered from that point forward and is still growing today.

And I had been given a unique and special gift for dealing with difficult and stress-causing employee issues—one that would stay with me, forever. Thanks, Jim, for uprooting and destroying that first stake in the ground and for driving an unmovable, much deeper one in its place.

KENT FRIEL AND JOE HARRISON

My career coaches at the time when I decided to leave Xtek and search for my first opportunity to run a business. It was 1998, and I felt as though I was ready to take on a head job. In exiting, I knew that I was assuming real risk, since I had no next job to go to. But I trusted my instincts that the time had come for me to strike out on my own. And I knew that my attitude and work ethic, two things I had been careful to keep always in focus—and to consciously develop throughout the course of my career—would serve me well in my pursuit of a new leadership role. My Xtek bosses blessed the move and allowed me to meet with and choose from among several outplacement firms as part of our separation agreement.

I chose a firm by the name of Schonberg and Associates, owned by Kent Friel. Joe Harrison was assigned as my personal coach. Through the several months of my job search, Joe and Kent kept me focused and enthused, and they helped me to evaluate and sort through the different opportunities that came my way. In the end, they were one of the major influences in my accepting the position to join Hydro Systems and Dover, the company from which I retired in 2015. Joe and Kent taught me to view opportunities from all sides, and not to put any one opportunity in a "box" based on type or size of company. They forced me to really think through the long-term implications of choosing my next employer, and to be honest when assessing the future potential of a business based on the strength of its people and its leadership – a way of thinking I was able to apply to great advantage during the later stages of my career. For their experience, thoughtfulness, consideration and candid (yes, even blunt) feedback, I will be forever thankful. Two outstanding and experienced professionals with whom I happened to intersect paths at precisely the moment I needed them the most.

JACK ROY AND GARY GOLUB

The owners of Hydro Systems, the company where I chose to work after leaving Xtek. Jack Roy is often referred to as the "modern-day founder" of the company. Jack bought the business when it was still in its infancy, grew it to nearly $20 million, and sold it to Dover. Gary Golub was Jack's business partner. I first met Jack and Gary in 1998, just about a year after they had sold their company to Dover. They (and Dover) were looking for someone to lead the business in its transition from private ownership; I was chosen and vetted over an intensive two-year period before being given the head job.

Jack and Gary ran the business with a firm focus on growth and profitability, but also on taking great care of their employees and customers. They had injected the entire workforce with an attitude of teamwork beyond anything that I had experienced to that point in my business career. Jack's fundamental business philosophy centered on treating people with respect and sharing the wealth of the enterprise with all of the employees of the company, something rarely seen in this day and age of "all about me" business ownership. A classically educated Harvard MBA, Jack had grown up within the IBM organization when it was one of America's proudest and most successful companies, and he had done extremely well in a number of senior-management roles. He decided to take his shot at the world of small business after leaving IBM, and he bought and sold several other companies prior to purchasing Hydro Systems.

It would be fair to say that Jack's fundamental business philosophy and attitude, more than any other, has impacted the way in which I manage and think about business. Focus on growth. Hire the best people. Trust the workforce and pay them fairly for improving and growing the company. Share the success and the financial rewards of the business with all employees.

Simple sounding, unyielding, stiff-character-requiring stuff. Particularly when everything you have done in your career has been wildly successful and the people around you are constantly reminding you just how brilliant you really are. I mean, think about it, how does an IBM guy, trained at one of the biggest of the big companies in the world, decide to adopt a philosophy around sharing the wealth of the enterprise with all his employees? The answer, of course, was that Jack had the strongly held personal belief—and the guts—to try it!

Jack and Gary instituted a program of profit-sharing, which, for the 17 years I worked at Hydro Systems, paid out an average of 15-20 percent in quarterly cash bonuses, on top of base salary. That means that an employee just starting with the company on the factory floor, and trying to raise his or her family on $25,000 per year, gets another $5,000 through profit-sharing. The key insight that Jack and Gary grasped (and that so many others in business today somehow seem to miss) is what a huge difference that kind of additional compensation makes to the average employee – a difference relative to what they are able to do for their families.

The extra pay derived from profit-sharing allows employees to deal with those unexpected expenses that always seem to creep into our lives, or to afford a vacation for the family that would otherwise have been out of reach. It means providing for a better future for their children. Starting a college-education fund or a savings plan for a grandchild. Those things we all want for ourselves and our families, and the reasons we all get up in the morning and go to work!

Profit-sharing is the employees' reward for helping to grow the company and make it more profitable, and there is no upper limit to the program. No big deal, you say? Well, just think, for a moment, about working as an engineer at Jack and Gary's company, where you make perhaps $80,000 per year in salary, but another *$16,000* in profit-sharing payments through the year. Are you going to work a little harder to get that critical, new product designed? Will your spouse understand when you have to stay late one evening to meet an important deadline for getting a new production tool launched? Will you answer the call from the factory, and with enthusiasm, when they need your help to design a new fixture that helps take a few minutes out of the time required to produce a particular item? Make that last-minute, unscheduled trip out of town to help a customer with a quality or installation issue? Support your sourcing team with drawing updates and revisions when they are trying to develop new suppliers?

You darn well bet you will. And guess what else you will do? You will ignore the constant calls from recruiters, promising you a better job and a brighter future at the company down the street.

On top of the profit-sharing program, Hydro Systems offered a full package of additional benefits, including fully paid health care, to all of its employees. You read that correctly. Fully. Paid. Health Care. As in, a dinosaur plan. As in, no one does that anymore. As in, huge differentiating factor in getting and keeping better employees than the competition. For the full 17 years I worked at Hydro Systems, we maintained at least one health-care plan that cost the employees nothing in annual premiums. Another simple, yet typically overlooked, opportunity learned from Gary and Jack – that doing the "little things" to demonstrate to employees that you have their best interests at heart, and treating them like true partners to your business success, will earn undying trust and loyalty. You get, and you keep, better people. Those better people produce better results. And, of course, the cycle feeds itself.

This type of benefit package and holistic view of the business also has a dramatic impact on day-to-day employee behavior. It creates an intense, positive climate of peer pressure, where the employee group tends to self-police. After all, people will simply not tolerate someone who is not pulling their weight, when they recognize that everyone is deriving benefit from the collective pool of profits generated by the performance of the business. (See Thing #3 for more on this aspect of how profit-sharing impacts company culture.) This leads directly to a unique, peer-influenced work ethic that permeates the culture of the organization and sustains itself without the need for any extraordinary push from management. Something every business owner would love to have woven into the fabric of his company!

But what's the ultimate measure to convince us that such an intensive cultural focus really does help in making a company more profitable?

Why, *results*, of course.

In the 17 years I worked at Hydro Systems, following and implementing Jack and Gary's system for running a great business, treating people well and sharing the wealth, we grew sales from less than $20 million to more than $100 million, EBIT (Earnings Before Interest and Taxes) from the mid-teens to almost 25 percent, and enterprise value from $25 million to $230 million. And, in 17 years, we rarely lost a key employee we didn't "want" to lose.

Brilliant senior management, you say? Secular tailwinds? Wildly expanding, protected, niche markets?

Nope. None of that. *Better, more dedicated, more loyal people.*

Thanks, Gary and Jack.

ANDY GALLIATH, BOB LIVINGSTON AND THE TRUE VALUE OF TEAMWORK

Andy Galliath is used here as a proxy for every great Dover operating company peer president with whom I had the honor to work during the years I was employed with Dover. Andy is a guy who sold his business to Dover and made a personal fortune on the sale. He figured he would retire after transitioning the business, but he ended up staying and working for another 10-15 years—well past normal retirement age. Andy remains a great friend, and he will tell you, flat out, that he stayed so long after the sale of his business because he loved the camaraderie and peer interactions that were so unique to Dover during the time he worked for the company. Andy was a great teammate—fun-loving, bright as all get-out, engaging, strategic. He had the whole package.

But it wasn't just Andy; it was the full set of peers with whom I had the pleasure of working during my many years at Dover. Hard-working, intelligent, generous people. Always ready to host your visit, share a best practice, lend you their talent, help you to become established in a new geography, do whatever it took to help you be more successful with your business. And having worked with and been around lots of big companies in my time, I can assure you, this is highly unusual behavior for a large, public corporation.

Of course, I could substitute any of dozens of names of Dover peers with whom I built close friendships in place of Andy's, and I would tell you that I feel much the same way about any of them. Dave Ropp, Dave Wightman, Rick Hajec, Bob Leisure, Carmine Bosco, Bill Strenglis, Jim Mitchell, Jim Kosh, Dan Newman, Rob Galloway, Lon Perry, Gary Rychley, David Crouse, Mike Savignac, Tim Warning, Bill Johnson, Andy Fincher, John Pomeroy, Paul Goldberg, Ray McKay, Steve Oden. And a dozen more whom I am certain I have missed. All great people. All smart people. And every one of them understood the extreme value of teamwork and of sharing the knowledge built-up in your business with others. It's what made Dover—at least for me—such an attractive place to come to work for, all those years ago.

Bob Livingston was the CEO at Dover for the final eight years I worked for the company. One of the most insightful, brilliant minds you will ever meet. Wildly successful business career, deep thinker, caring family man. A highly likeable guy. Bob taught me an interesting lesson relative to the strength and power of peer relationships and teamwork during the period of time when I reported directly to him, and while he was "on his way up" through the ranks at Dover. Bob had just inherited a rag-tag group of companies in his first divisional leadership role, including my company, Hydro Systems. He showed up at an annual plan presentation for Hydro in order to meet my staff and to become acquainted with our business model, and he asked me to stay after the presentation to have dinner.

Over dinner, we talked about teamwork, and Bob emphasized that he wanted me to become close to some of my more experienced teammates in the new division, believing it would be of great benefit to both the others and me. Like many of you, I had heard this sort of rah-rah speech before from newly appointed leaders, and so I nodded politely and figured I would return to Cincinnati and to Hydro Systems and get on with my job, allowing the others amongst my new peer set to do the same. Nice pep talk, Coach, now let me go do my own thing and those guys can go do theirs.

Well, I must tell you, a very strange thing happened upon my return home. There was a memo from Bob waiting for me, inviting me and my peers in the new group to a "get acquainted" meeting in New Hampshire, where the division for which Bob was responsible had its headquarters at the time. Nothing unusual about that, of course. Every new leader calls his troops together to talk business, early in his reign. It's a time to lay out the new guy's business habits, philosophy, expectations. And to review numbers. How is everyone doing against the business plan for the year? What's the short-term outlook? Any major changes to your strategy based on market developments? How are you looking against the latest, favorite Dover metrics (quite different, of course, from last year's favorites – you all know the drill)?

Problem was, that's not what the agenda described. Here is what it said, instead:

Monday evening: Arrivals and dinner with team

Tuesday morning, 8 a.m. to 9.a.m.: Who is Bob Livingston? Family, management style, work history

Tuesday morning, 9 a.m. to noon: Open discussion around your own business priorities (No metrics, no numbers, please. Let's just talk!)

Tuesday afternoon: Lunch and golf with team

Tuesday evening: Dinner with team

Wednesday morning: Departures

OK, I thought. Now, this is a bit different. Let's just see how it goes. And how it went was an absolute awakening. We spent 95 percent of our time together just getting to know one another. Business discussions were clearly and visibly prioritized behind just hanging out, becoming acquainted and having fun together. Bob treated us like honored guests, with great food, good wines, a beautiful golf course and nice cigars on the deck after supper. Certainly not what I expected, and a real eye-opener for me. This guy, it was immediately apparent, truly valued teamwork over everything else. He knew, it would seem, that if you build a high-performing team and work to make them trust one another, then good results would follow. But first, you need to build the team. Right off the pages of one of Patrick Lencioni's books. Amazing.

During my time working directly for Bob, I experienced many such meetings and many such non-traditional agendas, with the time slanted heavily toward building the team and treating people well. This, in large part, simply as thanks for the extraordinary efforts we all put in as Dover operating company leaders. Bob took us to The Homestead where we golfed, fished and shot sporting clays. He took us to the Calgary Stampede and to Banff, just to share a nice meal, hang out together, and experience the beauty of the Canadian Rockies. He took us to many other places where I had never been, and gave us the opportunity to experience things I had not yet experienced. We played cards at night. We drank wine. We smoked the occasional cigar. And Bob built one hell of a team.

Unfortunately, my time reporting to Bob was short, as he was moving fast up the food chain in Dover, but it was long enough to have the opportunity to learn the lessons from a master team-builder. And, for that, I will be forever thankful.

Good on ya, Bob.

FRAN NUNAN, STEVE VOGEL AND KEVIN GRACE
Fran, Steve, Kevin and I all worked closely together at Hydro Systems for many years. Fran led the HR team, Kevin was Vice President, North American Sales and Marketing, and Steve was my CFO and business partner. When I decided to take on the

daunting task of authoring this book, Fran, Steve and Kevin agreed to serve as my "inside team" of editors. Having lived through the lessons described within the book during our days together at Hydro, the group of them were uniquely qualified to help me tell the story in a way that captured the true spirit of the company and culture we all built, together.

They spent countless hours with me, through the summer and fall of 2015, improving and perfecting the manuscript for the book before I eventually passed it to Ann Weber for final editing and proofing. Fran, Steve and Kevin encouraged me to make many substantive changes to the book, which, I believe, have made it unimaginably better (and more fun to read). To these three great teammates, who took the time from their busy lives to help me tell the story accurately, and with passion, I will be forever thankful. The book is their work, as much as it is mine.

THE MOST IMPORTANT INFLUENCERS IN YOUR CAREER

So then, that's the list of the most important influencers on my career. All bright, thoughtful, kind people who were willing to give of their time and share their lessons so that I could adapt and improve my own approach to business, and to leading people. For the lessons that each of them taught me, I will be forever thankful. Their help and assistance to me, at the time when I needed it most, has helped me to help my own family in uncountable, lasting ways. I can think of no better gift to receive and to pass on to others.

I am certain that you, too, have such influencers in your life. People who have helped shape how you conduct business, treat and lead people, and relate to others both at work and at home. My simple advice to you? Thank them for all they have done for you, and thank them, *now*.

Don't wait to write your book.

CPSIA information can be obtained at www.ICGtesting.com
Printed in the USA
LVOW08*1254300916

506846LV00002B/4/P